Romper Room's Miss Sally Presents 200 Fun Things To Do with Little Kids

Romper Room's Miss Sally Presents 200 Fun Things To Do with Little Kids

SALLY CLASTER BELL

AND DOLLY LANGDON

A Dolphin Book
Doubleday & Company, Inc., Garden City, New York
1983

To my best teachers—
Jenny and Joe

Library of Congress Cataloging in Publication Data

Bell, Sally Claster.
Romper Room's Miss Sally presents 200 fun things to do with little kids.

Includes index.
1. Creative Activities and Seat Work.   2. Amusements.
3. Family Recreation.   I. Langdon, Dolly.   II. Title.
GV1203.G344   1982   790.1'922   AACR2
ISBN: 0-385-15735-5
Library of Congress Catalog Card Number 80–1807
Copyright © 1983 by Sally Claster Bell and Dolly Langdon

DESIGNED BY MARILYN SCHULMAN

Contents

CHAPTER TEN

Unbirthdays and Other Red-letter Days

A FAMILY CALENDAR—MOBILES FOR ALL SEASONS—COSTUMES FOR
ANY OCCASION—MAD HATTERS—BIRTHDAYS COME ONCE A YEAR—
UNBIRTHDAYS COME ANY TIME

AFTERWORD

Talking Back to Television

GAME PLANS FOR TV—ACTIVE TELEVISION VS. PASSIVE TELEVISION

Time Out for Kids

THIS IS A PRACTICAL BOOK FOR BUSY PARENTS like me, overscheduled parents who are both working at full-time jobs as well as raising a young family. Taking time out for my two children, twelve-year-old Jenny and eight-year-old Joey, is a top priority in my crazy daily schedule. But making that time count, making the hours I spend with my kids creative and just plain fun, is a constant challenge.

I think there are a lot of American families like mine—who wish they could buy watches with thirty-nine-hour days! Or mothers like me who secretly wish they could fit that "perfect mother" myth of always being there with rubbers when it rains and fresh-baked cookies after school. Or fathers who wistfully yearn to fit that picture of the "ideal daddy" who comes home every night at 6 P.M. to sit down at the head of the family dinner table.

But most of us have been forced to be more honest with ourselves. There are still only twenty-four hours in one day—and when you have to work and sleep, that doesn't leave too much time for having fun with the kids. Too often we waste the time we do find in predictable hassles: Whose turn it is to do the dishes? Whose favorite TV program are we going to watch? Who forgot to feed the dog? Even routine chores like going to the grocery store or buying shoes or driving a car pool can be eaten up in agonizing battles between a pressured parent and an obstinate five-year-old.

I think one of the secrets to enjoying your children is to do *anything* you can to eliminate those *predictable* scenes of conflict. Hire a baby-sitter or leave the child with a neighbor when you go to the supermarket if that trip is an inevitable struggle of "I want" and "No, you can't have." If you must, omit one or two things from your grocery list to afford the cost of the sitter. Not only will you preserve your peace of mind, but the time you save by shopping alone can be added to the time you've already set aside to do something that will be pleasant for both you and your child. I think sometimes parents forget that quality time spent with their kids should be fun for them, too!

I also firmly believe that a *practical* parent has a lot more fun than one who is constantly worrying about being *perfect*. Believe it or not, the store-bought cookies in a cellophane bag can taste just as good to a five-year-old as the ones you spent hours baking! And somehow the family doesn't fall apart if everybody eats dinner at a different time—especially if one child has gymnastics at 4 P.M., another has a soccer practice at 6 P.M., and a third has to start his homework at 7 P.M.—and Mommy and/or Daddy has to work late until 8 P.M. A child who has eaten a good meal when he was hungry is a lot more agreeable to be with when you finally do get home and have some time to spend with him.

If you can concentrate on doing away with even one of those struggles that seems to crop up in everybody's day, I think you will find you have more free time to do something with your child than you thought you did. You may have to revise some of your ideas about being a perfect parent—if, for example, you decide to stop arguing with your child about making his bed before he goes to school and spend that time reading to him instead. But if you never have time to read to him at bedtime, perhaps you should reevaluate your criteria for neatness. I don't think you will be dropping your standards. More than likely, you will be trading away tension for time.

In my eighteen years as a *Romper Room* teacher, I've discovered through trial and error a lot of ways to make those precious few hours set aside for kids more valuable. Some of the suggestions I'm going to make to you come directly from my experiences in working with children on the *Romper Room* television show. Because I have worked with literally thousands of children all over the world, I have had a chance to see children in new situations all the time—sometimes making them try things that are hard for them. I am able to see how they react and to ask them questions about what they think. And their answers are always brutally honest!

Over the years, it has become clear to me that even very young children are definitely more sophisticated, partly because of television, partly because changing family patterns and life-styles have made them more independent. The *Romper Room* staff at our head office in Baltimore is always researching and testing new games and projects that interest these changing children. And we're not just trying to be innovative. As a practical matter, we produce a daily television show five times a week fifty-two weeks a year. That means we must have enough material for 260 shows. And since each show features an average of seven segments, we must plan 1,820 segments a year!

Some of our segments present guests we think might be interesting for the children to meet— such as a bricklayer building a wall or an ice-skating family. We invite at least 125 guests each year to appear on the show. And some of our segments are action sequences—such as my visit to the San Diego Zoo or the Florida Sea World —which we occasionally repeat.

But many of our most successful and popular segments involve teaching the children a new concept (the metric system) or showing them how to make something (peanut-butter sculpture). Because our statistics show that our audience of preschoolers and their parents habitually watch *Romper Room* for two continuous years, we try to keep the teaching material fresh by not repeating those segments more than once a year. So we are constantly updating our files and looking out for new projects.

Also, because we are working within the time limit of a half-hour program, most of our activities have to be ideas that four- and five-year-olds (both the children on the show as well as those watching at home) can grasp quickly and easily.

More than any parent ever dreamed, we are literally conscious of making every *second* of expensive air time count!

There's no question that being on television five days a week is what many people would call a "high glamour" position. In order to bring more of the outside world into the *Romper Room* kindergarten, I travel a great deal to film sequences. In the past few years, I have traveled an average of 50,000 miles a year, including visits to dozens of cities across the U.S., a tour of Latin America, and stops in Canada and Europe. I not only get to meet celebrities, but am sometimes treated like one myself. Children who recognize me in an airport will stop me to say, "Hello, Miss Sally! I just saw you on TV!" And I do many personal appearances around the country where I meet and talk to older children as well as to little ones.

Some of my adventures have been hardly what you would expect on the agenda of a kindergarten teacher. For *Romper Room* shows I have driven a lunar rover at the Cape Canaveral Space Center, shaken tongues with a whale at Sea World, dressed up and performed as a circus ringmaster at Washington's Capital Center, and almost been lost to the clouds when I flew in a hot-air balloon!

But off the *Romper Room* set, I'm reminded every day at home that I'm in the same boat as a tremendous number of people. I'm still a working mother with young children who has only so many hours in a day to juggle a job and a family life. I still have the same problems, the same conflicts, the same guilt feelings, that millions of other parents do. In addition to working all day, I still have to run a house, cook dinner and clean up eventually, and make sure that the children are taken care of.

People often ask me how I manage such a complicated life. I think I manage with a lot of luck and a lot of organizing. I don't have a magic formula. But something must work right for me because the time I spend with my own kids still happens to be my best time—and the most fun.

And that's really why I wanted to write this book. Because my job does involve working with preschoolers, parts of my two worlds overlap. Both as a working mother and as a professional who has worked with children, I'm going to outline for you a number of time-saving ways to make the hours you can take out for your children more productive and enjoyable for both of you.

I do want to emphasize that this is not a book for just mothers, or even for just fathers. It is a book for *both* parents. It is also a file of suggestions for any adult who could use some ideas for fun things to do with kids. Those grown-ups include anybody in the support-system population that every young family must rely on today: the Beautiful Baby-sitter, the Devoted Grandparent, the Terrific Teacher, the Loyal Neighbor, even the Alternate Parent (any friend or relative who is willing to take over from time to time).

In a nutshell, effective parenting in the 1980s means being realistic about what time we have available for our children—and then making the most of it. So, I've organized the suggestions in this book into chapters that I hope will help busy adults squeeze more time for their kids into the most impossible and inflexible of schedules.

For starters, I'm sure you can find something to try in Chapter One, "Beat the Clock," where I've listed a different project for every hour of the day. If you can find only snatches of time each day for your kids, don't despair. Take a look at Chapter Two, "Easy Does It," for ideas that literally require fifteen minutes or less. If you and the children have to stay indoors, glance at Chapter Five, "Housebound?" for a list of inside activities.

I'd like to emphasize that you will have to spend very little money to try out these projects. Most of the items required for making things are already in your own house. Many of the activities we've practiced time and time again on *Romper Room*. Some ideas are drawn from my own personal experiences. And some of the best tips come from other parents who've discovered unusual ways to cope.

I've also included in an Afterword some thoughts about television watching for kids. Since none of us can avoid this extra family member who often presides over the living room, you might be interested in what some experts think about too much television and some ideas for developing critical viewing habits in very young children.

It's half-past twenty-seven o'clock tonight in my house in Baltimore. Today was a Saturday, so after lunch I found time to make a cereal box village with Joey from discards in our recycle box (see Chapter Four). Then Jenny and I spent some time outside together. My bicycle has a flat tire, so I jogged while she biked alongside. My favorite baby-sitter took over at 5:30 P.M. when two of Jenny's friends arrived to spend the night. I'm going to the movies later, so she and the girls heated a frozen pizza in the oven for everybody's supper. Now Jenny and her friends are playing a board game with Joey while I'm in the kitchen assembling the ingredients of my "Sunday Morning Sleep-in-late List" (see Chapter Seven). While the children are making their own breakfast tomorrow morning, I'll be sleeping until 11 A.M. And that's what I mean by being practical —instead of being perfect!

Sally Claster Bell

Romper Room's Miss Sally Presents 200 Fun Things To Do with Little Kids

Beat the Clock: One Day's Countdown

Preview:

HERE'S A FULL DAY'S WORTH OF FUN . . . FOURteen sure-fire projects that will occupy your child from before breakfast until after bedtime. From beanbags to butterflies to books to boats, every one has been a hit with *Romper Room* preschoolers, and since there's one for every hour of a kid's day, you'd have to be a busy parent indeed not to be able to fit at least one of them into your daily schedule.

For each project, you'll find a list of materials required, along with an estimate of the time you'll probably spend getting the child started.

Many of the projects found in these pages require the use of scissors. As a rule, when dealing with young children, it's best to use the not-too-sharp, blunt-tipped variety known as "safety scissors," even when an adult is doing the cutting. There will be times, however, when the use of sharp scissors is necessary—to cut heavy cardboard, for example. A few projects even call for X-acto or utility knives, which are very sharp and should *never* be left around unsupervised children. As with anything else that might injure a youngster, parental discretion is advised; when it comes to scissors, my motto is: Better safety than sorry.

Obviously, the times of day I've selected for some projects are interchangeable—depending on the mood and attention span of your youngster . . . and on your mood, too. Some, like the scarecrow, are activities that will call for your help—or at least your supervision. Others, like beanbag basketball, just about take care of themselves. Remember that most kids are more alert in the morning and are often tired and cranky in the afternoon. Five o'clock still tends to be the "ugly hour"—a time to avoid complicated directions and to choose something simple but creative that releases tensions, which you and your child will enjoy doing together.

As you read through the other chapters, try to keep your daily schedule in mind. No matter how little time you have available, you'll find a project here that you and your child can share. I doubt that anyone would want to try *all* of these ideas in one day, but don't ever say you couldn't think of anything to do.

7 A.M.   HOW TO TIE A BOW

Probably no skill gives a preschooler more pleasure and self-confidence than knowing how to tie his own shoes. It's often a mark of distinction among his peers who have to wait at nursery school for the teacher to tie them up.

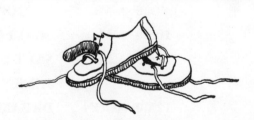

MATERIALS:
    shoes with laces
    shoe box top
    colored ribbon or yarn (2 colors)
TIME:
    5 minutes to demonstrate—lots of time to
    practice

Here's a project for any morning that will soon become a project for *every* morning. You can use this method with your child's shoes themselves. Or you can make a practice board out of a shoe box top with two different colored ribbons. If your little girl wears pigtails, make a fake braid out of yarn and let her practice on that. A box that looks like a present in need of a bow is another way to pique children's interest. As a rule, however, mastering shoelaces is every kid's number one goal . . . and a fine way to start the day.

This method is simple for children to catch on to, but make sure that you follow each step very,

very slowly. The first time around, demonstrate several times. Then help your child to practice; he'll need to try several times before the method becomes second nature.

If you are using a shoe box top, cut 2 small holes and pull the ribbon through. Explain to your child that to tie a bow, he is going to learn how to make two X's with the ribbon.

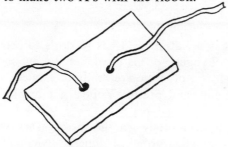

1. Cross the ribbon to make an X and curve one piece around and through the bottom of the X. Pull the two ends tight.

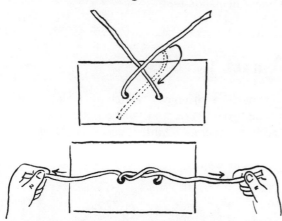

2. Take one piece of ribbon and loop it over your index finger with your other hand.

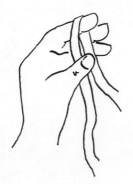

3. Loop the second piece of ribbon over your third finger.

4. Take one loop in each hand and cross them to form an X again.

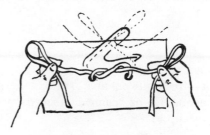

5. Take one loop and curve it over and through the bottom half of the X and pull tight.

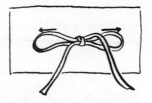

Now you have a bow! As you can see once you've practiced this method a few times, the second part of the bow tying is identical to the first part. Most children find the two X's easy to understand.

8 A.M.   BREAKFAST SUNDAE

What did parents do before yogurt was so easily available in so many flavors? Be sure to include it on your shopping list—it's one of the foods that little children usually like that is actually good for them!

MATERIALS:
  containers of vanilla and/or fruit-flavored yogurt
  fruit—fresh, if possible (there are always bananas), or canned (sliced peaches, pineapple)
TIME:
  5 minutes (plus a few minutes more if you want to show how to slice a banana or use a can opener on a tin of fruit)

This really is very close to a "do-it-yourself" job. Kids can make crazy fruit faces in yogurt—or free-form art will do just as well. To make his own sundae, all a child has to do is to choose a flavor of yogurt for his breakfast and put some in a bowl . . . or, if you're really in a hurry, use a paper cup, and presto! You've got breakfast to go.

If you can subtly get the message across that yogurt contains proteins, minerals, vitamins, fat, and sugar and that goodness is more than a matter of taste, you will be teaching your children a valuable lesson in nutrition as well as offering them a delicious treat.

9 A.M.   BEANBAG/TRASH-BALL BASKETBALL

Both of these "basketball" games can be played indoors or outdoors, and an active preschooler can burn up a lot of energy while Mom's busy with the breakfast cleanup. After you've set up the game, you can leave him to play alone . . . or you can join in for a little one-on-one.

Trash Balls

MATERIALS:
  newspaper
  masking tape
  wastebasket
TIME:
  10 minutes

Trash-ball basketball is lots of fun mainly because it gives children an excuse to do what they know they're not supposed to do—throw trash!

To make the balls, show your child how to crumple a sheet of newspaper into a ball shape. Make the ball firm by fastening it with a strip of masking tape. Let him make as many as he wants to—at least three or four, possibly a dozen.

Now take an empty wastebasket and set it up as the "goal." You and your child can take turns trying to "score." Children can play this game together, of course, making it a winner for birthday parties as well.

Beanbag Basketball

MATERIALS:
old socks
dried beans
rubber bands
cardboard box
crayons or Magic Markers
scissors
TIME:
20 minutes

You can make your own beanbags by filling old socks with dried beans from the supermarket. Knot the openings or fasten them with rubber bands.

If you aren't too energetic, you can again use a wastebasket as a "goal." But for extra flair, particularly at a party, use an old cardboard box to make a "Funny Face" target. Kids love to draw the face (but it's a lot easier if you supervise the cutting of heavy cardboard).

On the lid, draw big circles for eyes and a mouth, and then cut them out. Use crayons or Magic Markers to finish decorating the face— like a clown, for instance, with wavy eyebrows and a big red dot for a nose.

Then stand the lid up and secure it by placing the bottom of the box in the lid. For extra security, use masking tape to fasten the two pieces of the box together.

Now stand the "Funny Face" on a table and show your child how to toss beanbags through the eyes and mouth. This is more of a challenge to a youngster than using the wastebasket. To make the game more competitive, write numbers over each opening—giving a toss through the mouth more points than through the eyes.

NOTE: You can make a "Funny Face" out of a large grocery box by cutting out the eyes and mouth on one side.

10 A.M.   SCARECROW PAL

Once you've done the basics, a child can complete this scarecrow alone, but he's such a delightful character that you might enjoy sticking around to help make him come to life.

MATERIALS:
paper bag—lunch-bag size
string mop (child-sized is best), or yardstick
wire coat hanger
pipe cleaners or twist ties
rubber bands
newspapers
children's clothes:
overalls or jeans
long-sleeve shirt or jacket
ribbons and pins for suspenders
scissors
crayons or Magic Markers
TIME:
15 minutes to get started—30 minutes to complete

You will have to help assemble the scarecrow so that your child can dress him. First, poke the wire hanger hook through the middle of the mop

frame. Bend the hook a little to tighten it and fasten the hanger securely to the mop handle with a pipe cleaner, a twist tie, or a rubber band.

If you're using a yardstick, bend the hanger hook and wrap it as securely as you can around the stick about 8 inches from the top. Secure it with pipe cleaners, or, for extra strength, you can even use masking tape.

Now take the paper bag and the crayons or Magic Markers. Make a funny or sad face on the bag and slip it over the mop head. The strings of the mop will stuff the bag—if you're using a yardstick, your scarecrow will have a skinny face unless you stuff the bag with crumpled newspaper. Secure the "face" with a pipe cleaner. The scarecrow is ready to be dressed.

Show your child how to crumple the newspapers, and then stuff the clothes after fastening the ends of the shirt sleeves and pant legs with rubber bands. Next, dress the hanger and mop handle in the stuffed clothing, making sure that the mop handle lies along the inseam of one trouser leg.

Overalls work best on the scarecrow because the shoulder straps will keep them up. If you use jeans, make suspenders out of ribbon and pin them to the waistband.

Finally, cut a slash about 3″ long across the top of the paper bag "forehead" and pull some mop strings through for the hair. Put a hat on the scarecrow and your child has a new pal for the day!

11 A.M.   EVERYONE CAN BE AN ARTIST: SALT-DOUGH PLAQUES AND JUNK SCULPTURE

If you're at home at eleven o'clock, chances are you can spend an hour on these projects. Both challenge a child's imagination and sense of play. Everyone is successful at this!

Salt-dough Plaques

MATERIALS:
- 1 cup flour
- ½ cup salt
- a little less than ½ cup water
- poster paint or Magic Markers or watercolors
- brushes

What you're aiming for here is an impression of your child's hand—a clay plaque which will not only delight the two of you, but which can also make a memorable present for a lucky relative.

To make the "clay," mix the flour and the salt in a bowl. Add water until the mixture holds together like dough. Knead 4 minutes, and you're all set to go. (This dough will keep five days in the refrigerator if stored in plastic wrap.)

Take a ball of dough and flatten it into a circle about ½″ thick. Lightly flour your child's hand and have him press it into the circle until it makes a clear impression in the dough. If you want to hang the plaque later, now is the time to punch a hole with a toothpick up at the top above the fingers. Use the rest of the dough to make as many more impressions as your child wants.

Once the plaque is completed, it must dry, making this an ideal project to extend over a period of days. Place the finished work on a cookie rack and let it sit in the open air for at least 48 hours. The dough will dry white and hard. When it's dry, you might remind your child how soft it was when he made the plaque.

When they're dry, the plaques can be left plain —or decorated with watercolors, Magic Markers, or poster paint. Why not a hand covered with rings? Or a green-monster hand? Encourage your child's imagination to wander.

A youngster who enjoyed making these plaques might like to do one for each member of his family—for a "family of hands." (Once the dough is made, a child can make a plaque like this without assistance. It will be a permanent statement of himself at this age.)

Junk Sculpture

This creative project uses household odds and ends to produce an unusual and unique piece of artwork that will appeal not only to children, but often to adults as well.

MATERIALS:

    wood scraps, old spools, bottle caps, and other small objects
    Elmer's glue
    paintbrush
    heavy cardboard or poster board

TIME:

    30 minutes to 1 hour

Spread out the various objects on a worktable. The more shapes and sizes—within reason, of course—that you can find, the more fun it will be for your child. Have the Elmer's glue ready in a bowl as well as a paintbrush to apply it with. You should also precut the cardboard—the side of a grocery box will do nicely. Be sure to make it a workable size, at least 8″ × 10″.

Use the paintbrush to spread the cardboard thoroughly with Elmer's glue. Then turn your child's imagination loose to choose pieces to stick on the "picture." You may need to use extra glue to make some objects stick firmly.

These sculptures really can be *very* dimensional. Encourage your child to see spatial relations and to build up and even extend out from the cardboard.

Like the salt-dough plaques, junk sculpture can, of course, be painted, but this is best left for another day, when the glue has dried completely.

You will be amazed at how effective and elegant these pieces can be. I have one from my Jenny that is not only five years old but does double duty as a last-minute dining room centerpiece. Tuck in two or three marigolds, and even your mother-in-law will ooh and ahh

12 NOON: DREAMY CREAMY SANDWICHES

There is, of course, nothing like little kids and their yen for peanut butter. But for a tasty change, here's a recipe for a simple sandwich kids can make for themselves. It is also extra nutritious.

MATERIALS:

    4 slices whole wheat bread
    3 ounces softened cream cheese
    1 tablespoon jelly
    1 large banana
    2 large tablespoons chopped nuts

TIME:

    10 minutes

Before you start, be sure the cream cheese has stood at room temperature for an hour to soften. Help your child spread two slices of bread with the cheese. Then let him spread the jelly on top of the cheese. After he has peeled the banana, lend a hand by slicing it into thin pieces. Show him how to arrange the slices on top of the jelly. For a flourish, let him sprinkle the chopped nuts on top of the bananas. Finally, let him place the two plain slices of bread on top of the slices with the filling. Show him how to cut the sandwiches into quarters to serve. Makes 2 sandwiches (8 quarters).

For your information, and to pass along to your child if you feel like it, this sandwich contains something nutritious from each of the four daily food groups:

DAIRY: Cream cheese
FRUIT: Banana
PROTEIN: Nuts
CARBOHYDRATES: Bread

1 P.M.   WINGS ON YOUR FEET—AN EASY BUTTERFLY

In lots of homes, naptime comes right after lunchtime, but if not, here's a quiet project that is always fun and guaranteed to be successful.

MATERIALS:
paper—any kind that is at least big enough for your child to stand on (newspaper, wrapping paper, construction paper, even a grocery bag)
crayons or Magic Markers
scissors
child's shoes
pipe cleaners (optional)
glue (optional)
TIME:
10 minutes

Place your child's shoes on the paper so that the toes are facing outward and the sides are touching. Use a crayon or Magic Marker to trace the outline of the shoes into the shape of a butterfly. Remove shoes and draw antennae on the outline. Color the butterfly and cut it out.

You and your child might want to make several of these winged creatures to decorate the walls of his room. If he likes the butterfly idea, you can be more ambitious in your embellishments: attaching pipe cleaners for antennae (just poke tiny holes in the top of the paper shape) and cutting out colored circles from scraps of construction paper or old magazines to glue on the wings for spots. This is an easy project for several children to do together.

2 P.M.   TRIPLE-THREAT DRAGON

Here's something to do when company comes—a homemade version of the dragon you and your child may have seen in a Chinese New Year parade, a colorful segmented body carried by dancers so that only their legs show.

MATERIALS:
3 (or more) brown boxes from the supermarket, large enough for a child to fit under. Flaps should be removed.
heavy string or twine (clothesline works best, if you have some extra)
scissors
crayons or Magic Markers
TIME:
20 minutes to make together

To make your dragon scary, draw a face with big, blazing eyes on the first box. Cut eyeholes so that the child can see out for safety.

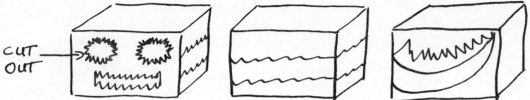

On the second box, draw the horned part of the dragon's back to represent the body. Cut side peepholes so that the child who gets inside can see out.

On the third box, draw a large, curling tail. Again, remember to cut peepholes.

To link the boxes, poke holes in each one through which to run the clothesline or string. You'll need 1 hole in the back of the first box, 2 holes in the second—front and back—and 1 hole in the front of the last box. Push the clothesline through the holes, and knot it to tie the boxes together. Now you've got a three-man dragon that can walk, dance, or crawl on the floor.

You can always add more boxes to the body and the tail of the dragon—one for every child. This is a great project for any time when you have a group of children: at play school, at a birthday party, or after school.

3 P.M.   STAINED-GLASS WINDOWS

MATERIALS:
newspapers
waxed paper squares cut the same size (6″ × 6″ is a good size to work with)
iron

crayons
table to iron on
shredded leaves, bits of paper, etc., in bowls
scissors

TIME:
30 minutes

Since this project involves an adult using an iron, it is definitely something you have to do together. Try this project when you won't be rushed. The results are worth it.

Spread the newspaper on the table (this keeps wax from coming off on the table when you iron). Then place a piece of the waxed paper on the newspaper with the waxy side up. Let the child put bits of shredded leaves, yarn, string, etc. on the surface of the waxed paper in any random way (or he can make a scene if he likes).

Now show your child how to make crayon shavings by using the blade of safety scissors against the sides of the crayons. Put different colors in different bowls.

The next step is really fun. Kids love to arrange the crayon shavings on specific sections of the waxed paper—by color. (Don't overlap colors, or you'll have a mess!) To seal the "window," place a second square of waxed paper, waxy side down, on top of the arrangement. Cover all with a piece of newspaper.

Now, while your child watches, run your iron (set it at a low temperature) over the newspaper several times to melt the crayon shavings inside. When you have finished, *voilà!* A picture that looks like stained glass. To make the "window" even more permanent, neater, and suitable for hanging, stick a border of Scotch or colored tape around the edges.

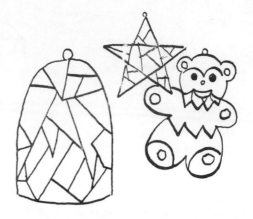

NOTE: Squares are easiest to work with the first time. On another go-around, you can try cutting the waxed paper into any shape for even more striking effects. Cut an arched shape like a church window, for example. Or, why not try stars and animal shapes (traced from cookie cutters or patterns in coloring books)? The latter, by the way, are unusual additions to a Christmas tree.

---

4 P.M.   BODY PICTURES

These unusual likenesses are sometimes as much fun for grandparents (especially those who live far away) to receive as photographs. Once you get the kids started, this is also a good project to keep them entertained while you are fixing dinner.

MATERIALS:
    large sheet of brown wrapping paper slightly
        larger than your child (probably at least
        4' long)
    crayons or Magic Markers
TIME:
    15 minutes to start

You will be drawing a full-sized silhouette of your child. Ask him to lie down flat on the paper so that you can draw an outline picture of him. Make sure that he arranges his arms and legs so that you can trace around his entire body with the Magic Marker or crayon. When you have finished, hold the paper up so that the child can see "himself." Then let him draw in with crayons or markers facial features and clothing. (To make drawing easier, make sure the paper is on a hard flat surface, such as a floor without a rug; or, Scotch tape the paper temporarily to a wall.)

Body pictures can be rolled up and tied with ribbon for presentation as a gift. A child might enjoy making one on his birthday and saving it until the next year to see how much he has grown. Several body pictures could also make a

mural in a child's room that he could continue to draw on. This project can work well, too, in the early morning to keep kids busy while you are making beds and breakfast. Trace the outline the night before, and let them amuse themselves with the coloring when they wake up.

5 P.M.   STROKING A PRESCHOOLER'S EGO: THE "ME" BOOK

Even very young children will enjoy making a book about themselves. This is an ongoing project that you can start one afternoon and return to time and time again. It's good for any quiet time—before naptime, before bed, and especially during the 5 P.M. "ugly" hour. You'll be making a kind of preschooler's diary—a special place for him to paste pictures he has drawn that he is proud of or pictures from magazines that appeal to him.

MATERIALS:

   2 pieces of construction paper or shirt cardboard for covers of a homemade scrapbook

   drawing paper cut or sized to fit between the covers

   crayons or Magic Markers

   old magazines

   scissors

   glue stick

   string or yarn (for tying pages together)

TIME:

   10 minutes to an hour

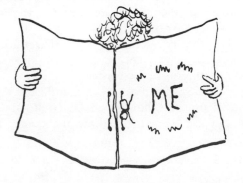

Perhaps you have an old scrapbook at home or can pick up an inexpensive one at the dime store. Better yet, make your own with construction-paper covers and drawing-paper pages. Punch 3 holes in the covers and tie the book together with yarn.

Help your child to write the word "Me" on the cover and suggest that he draw a picture or find one from a magazine to glue on the front of the book. You might even have a photograph of him that he could put on the cover.

What to put inside is entirely up to you and your child. Don't worry about logic or order. Some children like to use this for momentoes—pictures they have drawn at school, a pretty leaf, a snapshot of a friend, a birthday card, a ribbon from a present, a joke they like to tell (you may have to write this down for him).

Others can while away hours just looking through magazines and cutting out pictures for pasting in the book. You can give some guidance, for example, by suggesting that your child look for pictures of animals—as a way to learn their names and to become interested in knowing more about different animals. Or, tell him to look for pictures of other children. No matter what he cuts out, any picture can be the inspiration for making up a story when the two of you later look through the book.

As the "Me" book grows, you can use it as something to talk about together. Ask him to tell you why he has selected what he has—and you might be on the way to some revealing conversations about what goes on inside that pre-schooler's head.

6 P.M.   VEGETABLE PEOPLE

Some children take to eating vegetables with no fuss at all. But others would just as soon grow to adulthood on a diet of cold cereal and ice cream. One way to create interest in vegetables and give good nutrition a boost is to give them a little personality.

MATERIALS:
   vegetables, especially of odd shape or color
   toothpicks
TIME:
   10 minutes

Next time you go to the supermarket, keep an eye out for unusual-looking vegetables that can trigger your child's imagination. Cucumbers, eggplant, bumpy potatoes, green tomatoes, red onions, oversized radishes—all of them can have short lives as people or animals before going into the dinner salad.

For example, a cucumber makes a dashing dinosaur. Using toothpicks, add small green tomato legs, an undersized potato nose, and a radish tail.

When green peas are in season, make animals and men to ride them by sticking peas on toothpicks. Join the different parts of the body with more toothpicks.

Carrots make good bodies for men with celery arms and legs, and small potato heads. Turnips work in well, too.

An eggplant makes a wonderful giant head. You can attach bits of carrots or radishes for features, or even carve it like a pumpkin.

Children may or may not want to eat their vegetable creations, but you can take the opportunity to teach them the names of the vegetables and what favorite recipes they're used in. Whether they're stored in the refrigerator for snacking or used later in an adult meal, they need not, of course, be wasted.

At Thanksgiving time, take a little extra time to show the kids how to make potato turkeys. You can use them to decorate the dinner table with a seasonal touch.

MATERIALS:

    oval-shaped, medium-sized potatoes
    toothpicks
    construction paper
    feathers or cupcake liner for wings and tail

Although turkeys have only two legs, explain to the kids that the potato version needs three toothpicks to stand up. Insert them in the bottom of the potato. You'll find that the heavier they are, the better.

Draw a turkey head on stiff brown or white construction paper. Color it, cut it out, make a vertical slit in one end of the potato, and insert the head.

If you can find some small chicken feathers, stick these in the other end of the potato for the tail. You may need to make holes with a toothpick first. For wings, stick feathers in the sides of the potato.

Ruffled paper cupcake liners are a good substitute for feathers. Cut one in half for the tail. Make a gash across the end of the potato, being careful not to cut off the tail, and insert the cupcake liner. For wings, cut 2 wedges of cupcake liner and fasten them in place on the sides of the potato with toothpicks.

7 P.M.   BATHTUB FLOTILLA

Children who like to play in the bathtub can have great fun making fleets out of the four boats that follow.

Soap Sailboat

MATERIALS:

    a bar of floating soap
    toothpick
    scissors
    paper—square piece
    Scotch tape or glue

TIME:

    5 minutes

Lest your young yachtsman try to transform all the soap in the house into boats, you might tell him that only certain kinds of soap float.

To make the boat, begin with the sail. Explain that a sail usually has three sides. Then cut the square piece of paper from corner to corner and you will have 2 triangles. Use one of these triangles for the paper sail.

Tape or glue the sail to the toothpick—which will be the boat's mast. Push the mast firmly into the middle of the soap bar—and sail away!

Nut-shell Boat

MATERIALS:

    1 half walnut shell (meat removed)
    clay
    small straight stick or toothpick for mast
    scissors

TIME:

    5 minutes

Press a wad of clay into the nut shell. Cut the

paper into the desired shape for the sail, or use a pretty leaf. Poke the toothpick or the stick through the sail and press the end of the mast into the clay. These are very natural-looking boats, and are fun to sail outside in puddles, too, as well as in the tub.

Pea-pod Rowboat

MATERIALS:
  1 pea pod
  2 peas
  3 toothpicks
  1 small piece of cardboard (a matchbook cover is handy)
  scissors
TIME:
  10 minutes

Open a long side of a pea pod. Take out the peas. Now cut a little seat from the cardboard and place it in the "boat." It will keep the sides of the pod in position.

To make a little man to ride in the boat, use 2 peas, one for the head, and one for the body. Stick a toothpick through the peas and then stick the point of the toothpick into the little cardboard seat. Stick toothpicks into the bottom of

the pea. These will be the oars with which the little man rows the boat.

To make sure the pea-pod boat floats, attach a piece of adhesive tape or Scotch tape along the bottom of the pod to keep out the water.

These boats are so easy you will want to make several at a time.

Matchbox Sailing Regatta

MATERIALS:
  matchboxes (about 2″ size)
  toothpicks
  Scotch tape
  2 colors of construction paper
  scissors
TIME:
  10 minutes

Cut a triangle from one piece of the paper and tape it on a toothpick to make a sail. Then tape the bottom of the toothpick to the inside "front" of the matchbox. Make another sailboat with another color sail in the same manner.

To stage your own sailboat race, place the two boats in the water—and blow at the sails! Obviously, this regatta can be held in a dishpan as well as in a bathtub.

8 P.M.   YOUNG MAGICIAN

This is a magic trick that takes some practice— exactly the kind of thing to work on just before bed, or even a couple of times *in* bed. It creates the illusion that a big coin can pass through a small hole. Nothing messy here to dirty up sheets and blankets, just a piece of paper and a coin.

MATERIALS:
  sheet of construction paper
  a coin (preferably a large one, such as a fifty-cent piece)
  scissors
  pencil

Fold the paper in half and crease firmly. Then open the paper and place the coin in the center of the paper on the fold. Trace around the coin to make a circle. Now cut out a smaller circle within the traced outline. You should have a hole that is about ½–¾ the size of your coin.

To perform the trick, place the coin back inside the folded paper so that it is resting on the hole. Then take hold of the paper on the folded corners, thumbs in front, fingers in back close to the edges. Now bend the paper into a curved shape by bringing your thumbs forward toward each other. The motion will enlarge the diameter of the hole so that the coin will fall through.

Try this trick a few times yourself before teaching it to your child as you may have to enlarge the hole to allow the coin to fall through easily. When you have done it a few times in slow motion, you'll find the movement simple—and easy for a child to catch on to.

After a bit of nighttime practice, your young magician can confound the audience at the breakfast table the next morning. He should ask if anyone can put the coin through the hole without tearing the paper or enlarging the hole. When no one is able to, your child can perform the trick—and maybe teach it to his friends, too.

CHAPTER TWO

Easy Does It:
Only Fifteen Minutes
a Day

Preview:

KEEPING IN TOUCH

COMING AND GOING

SPEEDY SNACKS

PAPER QUICK TRICKS

TOP-SPEED PROJECTS

RAPID GARDENER

JUST BEFORE BED

THIS CHAPTER (AND THE NEXT) IS A PUSH FOR "quality time"—even if it comes in tiny fifteen-minute snatches. If you think a quarter of an hour couldn't possibly be long enough to amount to anything important, ask the following question of yourself and of your adult friends: What are the things you remember most vividly that you did *regularly* with your parents? Chances are you'll run into answers such as, "My mother *always* fixed my breakfast," or "My father *always* read me a bedtime story." You may also hear something colorful: "My father took me salmon-fishing in Alaska" or "My mother took me into barns to look for antiques." But rarely is the memory spectacular. More often it's a mundane routine—something you probably didn't even notice very much until you stopped to think about it many years later.

I'd like to underscore that word *routine* as a way of feeling connected to your kids. Most important to little children in feeling close to parents who often must spend more time away from home than they would like to is the certainty that there are some rituals they can count on—and even look forward to—even if they only last fifteen minutes a day. It's not the flashy present or the expensive outing, but often the humdrum yet regular things you can find to do together that make your relationship with your children special.

I suppose I'm old-fashioned enough to believe that if your time is short, it is best spent on one of the three "b's" that are part of every pre-schooler's day—breakfast, bathtime, and bedtime. Usually, one of these can fit into your schedule—and knowing you'll be there gives reassurance to a young child who may spend most of the day in someone else's care.

If you're looking for something more specific to label as "your thing"—as opposed to what others may be doing with your kids while you are away—this chapter contains a list of more than twenty easy, no-fuss projects that you can plan with your child. Just remember that the point of any project is not necessarily to complete something that you can hang on the wall, but to enjoy that time—however brief—that you can carve out to be together.

And one final word of caution. On those days when your time is literally limited to minutes, try at all costs to avoid spending the time reciting a litany of "don'ts" and "did you's?" Too often I find myself rushing in and starting to say: "Did you do your math, cover your notebook, pay the teacher back, call your grandmother?" Without stopping for air, I go on to, "Don't forget to wash your hair, feed the guinea pigs, don't wear that ripped shirt until I mend it, don't eat the strawberries—they're for company."

You can't blame the kids for tuning out if you habitually use up their valuable time with you scolding and reminding. Whenever you can, relegate the daily "have-tos" to a list (for non-readers, a picture list) that can be checked off while you are away from home. Then spend the time together doing something you both enjoy.

KEEPING IN TOUCH

Look at it this way. There are 1,440 minutes in a day. Surely you can set aside 15 of those precious minutes to remind your child you are thinking of him—even if you are away most of the day. If you can't be there in person, do the obvious—write or phone—but with a little imagination.

Pen-pal Postcards

Most of us like to send "wish you were here" postcards or "envy cards"—as one of my good friends nicknames them—to those back at home when we are away on trips. But what about being a pen pal with your child when you are away all day at work? Next time you are at a newsstand—or in an art museum—pick up a dozen postcards with bright pictures on them that you think your child might find appealing. It only takes a few minutes to write an address and dash off a brief message.

Everyone loves to get mail, and preschoolers are no exception—especially when they know the letter carrier comes every day. Even if your child is too young to read (perhaps someone at home can do that—or you can do it when you get home), he will like the picture, and it will give you something to talk about when you do come home.

Most important, is that a child is reminded an absent parent is thinking of him. I first learned this easy way of keeping in touch when I was away at camp. My dad was a very busy man, but he still used to write me every day. About half the time he dictated notes to his secretary which ended up "Sincerely, Bert" instead of "Best love, Dad." But I didn't care. I knew he was taking the time to dash off what I fondly came to call "milk-and-juice letters."

One of my best friends at camp received a postcard from her mother almost every day. Her mother was ambitious enough to have found all of her cards at the National Gallery of Art in Washington—so the daughter pinned up the postcards in our bunk room. By the end of camp, she had a wall full of pictures, a smattering acquaintance with some good art, and was definitely the envy of all the other kids waiting eagerly at mail time for some word from home.

Home Message Center

Use your bulletin board or chalkboard at home as a way of keeping in contact—especially if you have to leave home before your child gets up, are not there when he comes home from school, or come home after he has gone to bed.

Leave him a note in an envelope to be opened at one of those times when you are not there. And encourage him to pin things up during the day for you to find when you come home. When children have a working mother and father, using the message center can be more practical than just a place to pass love notes. Leave reminders to each other there ("we're out of cat food!" from a child who feeds the pets—or "take out the trash!" from an off-to-work mom or dad).

COMING AND GOING

Why not make a mini-ritual out of your arrival and departure from home?

What's In the Pocket—or the Pocketbook?

This is an easy game to play when you come home that can become an amusing routine. Children love the mystery of pockets. Empty the change in your pocket and teach your child the shapes of a penny, a dime, a nickel, and a quarter.

Another variation—based on the old Art Linkletter *Houseparty* game—give your child a list of three things to find in your pocketbook. A pencil, a lipstick, a ring of keys for example. Maybe tuck in a surprise for him—a roll of lifesavers, some peanuts in the shell, a piece of fruit. (Some parents might object to this, but the idea of the search—as a little fun game to play that belongs to the two of you—seems to work.)

Saltbox Bank

Give your child a place to store the change he collects from your pocket by showing him how to recycle an old saltbox into a homemade bank.

MATERIALS:

    1 empty saltbox
    construction paper
    glue stick
    scissors
    crayons
    coins

To make the bank more personal, cut a piece of construction paper to cover the saltbox. Glue it on, then let your child color it with decorations as he likes. The metal pourer makes a convenient money slot, or you can cut a larger slit in the top of the box.

Whenever you can find a few pennies, nickels, or dimes in your pocket for your child, encourage him to put them in the bank. Pennies-a-day thriftiness will pay off when the box is full. Then the two of you can open it and count the change. If your child is old enough to understand about "real" banks, you may want to help him open his own savings account. He will also surely be interested in a trip to the toy store to spend some of his stored-up riches.

Coin Rubbings

Here's a simple way to help children learn the names of the coins—by making pictures of them from rubbings, just as Colonial children often made pictures of things.

YOU WILL NEED:

    1 quarter, 1 nickel, 1 dime, 1 penny
    a pencil
    several sheets of fairly thin paper (typing
       paper works well)

After identifying the quarter, place it on a flat surface like a desk. Place the paper over the coin. Using the side of the pencil lead, show your child how to rub the lead gently over the coin. The picture of the coin and the size of the coin should come out on the paper.

Repeat the process with the other coins. Then finish up by writing beneath each coin picture the number of its cent value. (You might point out to your child, however, that the size of a coin is not consistent with its value in cents.) Kids can practice what they have learned by matching real coins to the paper shapes to review the names and values.

SPEEDY SNACKS

If mealtimes are frantic for you during a busy week, try one of these simplified routines.

The Night Before Breakfast . . .

Is a good time to set out what you will need to make things go smoothly in the kitchen on a busy workday/schoolday morning. A preschooler can make this one of his routine responsibilities —helping you plan the breakfast and setting the table. One of the charming scenes in the 1979 film *Kramer vs. Kramer* was the sight of six-year-old Justin Henry preparing breakfast while his dad shaved (simple fare of doughnuts and milk, but a small child was doing his part).

Breakfast is also a good time to learn about table setting since in most families it is a less complicated meal than others. Also, if you have more than one child, the breakfast detail is a routine even the youngest preschooler can handle by himself.

To help him out, you might make a chart for the refrigerator door with pictures of what you usually put out for breakfast. For example, on a sheet of paper paste pictures of:

    a cereal box
    sugar and creamer
    salt and pepper shakers
    a placemat with paper napkins and cutlery
        set out

If you practice this routine with your child a few nights before breakfast, he can then do it all by himself—with pride and pleasure.

Bedtime Cereal Snack

You may have an urge for a Reuben sandwich or a banana split just before bed, but here's a recipe for an easily made snack that will be bet-ter for you—and good for your child any hour of the day.

FOR ABOUT TWO QUARTS:
    1 box unsweetened dry cereal (your choice; we like Golden Grahams)
    1 cup shredded coconut
    1 box raisins
    1 can peanuts or soy nuts
    use your imagination for extras: dried apples or apricots, banana chips, date pieces, wheat germ

Mix the ingredients together in a large bowl. Then store the snack in a tightly covered container (preferably unbreakable plastic since little hands have a habit of digging in).

Timmy Tomato

We have had good luck on the *Romper Room* show with two particular vegetable people: Timmy Tomato and Susie Celery. Both of these foods are ones children encounter frequently. They can also both be eaten without cooking. A child who knows Timmy or Susie is waiting for him in the refrigerator might be tempted to choose them instead of other snacks.

To make Timmy Tomato, decorate one tomato with a celery mouth, carrot eyes, and hair made from celery leaves. Use toothpicks to attach the features.

If your child is intrigued by Timmy, you can use this opportunity to tell him some things about tomatoes:

    that they are fruits (cut open another tomato to show him the seeds)
    that they come in different sizes (this is easy

during the summer if you have a garden; you can also show him some cherry tomatoes if you have them in your market)

that they sometimes have different colors (show him a green tomato or a yellow one), but are most often red

that they contain an invisible vitamin—vitamin C—that helps keep our body tissues healthy

You can also go through your cupboard shelves and remind him of the many ways we eat tomatoes and the many dishes they are used in:

raw wedges in salads

cooked tomatoes in spaghetti sauce or pizza sauce

cooked tomatoes in ketchup for hamburgers and hot dogs

cooked tomatoes in vegetable and tomato soups

Timmy Tomato isn't guaranteed to make your child want to gobble up every tomato in sight—but as with most foods, especially unfamiliar ones, knowing something about the food and how it is used can make a child less dubious of what he might automatically reject as "yucky."

Susie Celery

Susie is somewhat harder for a child to make by himself the first time. But the idea here is again to create interest in a vegetable food that is low in calories and full of vitamins and minerals. Celery sticks are also ideal for spreading with other good things—such as peanut butter, cream cheese, tuna fish salad, and egg salad. If you can tempt your child to use celery instead of

crackers for spreads, you will be helping him to establish a good habit that many weight-conscious adults wish they had learned a long time ago.

To make Susie Celery, decorate a piece of cleaned celery (but don't cut off the top leaves) as illustrated below.

After your child has met Susie, you can use other cut celery sticks and show him how to spread them with cream cheese or peanut butter. (Crunching is good for teeth, too.)

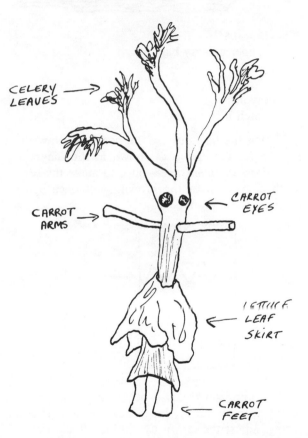

CELERY LEAVES →

CARROT ARMS →

← CARROT EYES

← LETTUCE LEAF SKIRT

← CARROT FEET

PAPER QUICK TRICKS

A piece of paper, scissors, crayons, glue, or Scotch tape—that's all you need to be endlessly inventive when you have a few minutes to spend with your child. Here are some very, very easy things to do with paper to warm you up.

Paper Crowns—King or Queen for a Day

If you come home carrying a bag full of groceries, here's a surprise you can help your child to make after you have put the food away.

MATERIALS:
  1 paper grocery bag
  pencil
  scissors
  crayons
  Scotch tape

Flatten the bag and use the pencil to draw the pattern for the crown as shown in the diagram. Cut across the bag twice—once to make the sawtooth edged top of the crown—and once again to make the bottom edge.

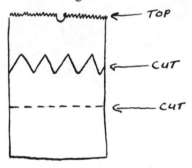

Depending on the size of the bag, the crown may be too big for the lucky new royalty. After a fitting, adjust the crown by cutting off the excess length and reattaching the ends with Scotch tape. Let your child use the crayons to add "jewels" if he wishes. Aluminum foil cutouts also add elegance.

Folded "A," "B," "C" Flags

If you have a flag reference book at home, you might enjoy making with your child these easy folded paper flags. You can make international naval code flag signals or flags for different countries. If you don't have a code book, try these patterns for easy flags representing "A," "B," and "C."

MATERIALS:
  sheets of paper (typing paper is fine)
  crayons
  scissors

To make the flag for the letter "A," fold a sheet of paper in half. Unfold the paper, and cut a triangle out of one half. Color white and blue as in the picture below.

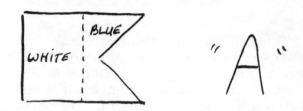

To make the "B" flag, use the same folding and cutting procedure. This flag, however, should be colored solidly red.

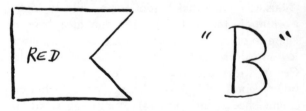

To make the "C" flag, pleat the paper in 5 folds from the short end. Color red, white, and blue as in the diagram below.

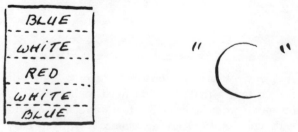

These flags can be made in miniature for the boats in your bathtub flotilla (see Chapter One).

TOP-SPEED PROJECTS

Show off a little bit. Help your child to make the following projects in fifteen minutes or less. Then he can teach them to his friends.

Binoculars

For these "high-powered glasses" you need:

2 empty toilet paper rolls
Scotch tape or masking tape
crayons or Magic Markers

Place the rolls side by side. Tape them together at both ends and in the middle. Let your child use the crayons and markers to decorate them, if he wishes. Then, take a look! Children who have made these binoculars on *Romper Room* like to look through their "glasses" and take turns telling about the "wild animals" they imagine they can see!

Happy Hands and Feet People

To make these imaginative creatures, all you need are sheets of drawing paper (any size, but at least as large as your child's hands and feet—old newspapers would even do) and crayons or Magic Markers.

Start with the hands. Show your child how to place one of his hands flat on a piece of paper. With his other hand, help him to trace the outline of the flat hand. Then show him how he can make a face with the crayon on the palm outline. The "fingers" can then be transformed into wild stand-up hair, an Indian headdress, and so on. Once he has the idea, let him trace more outlines and invent other "people."

For the "feet fellows," follow the same procedure, showing your child how to stoop with a foot flat on a piece of paper so that he can trace the outline of his shoe. Again, give him a few hints by drawing in the details of the first "foot face" yourself. Then he can take over, drawing and decorating as many feet people as he wants to.

Shoe Animals

If the "feet people" are a hit, try these shoe animals. You will need larger pieces of paper for the animals—so that you can add long limbs

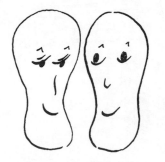

"Please draw me a hat—my head is cold!"

such as the neck of a giraffe or the trunk of an elephant.

Again, show your child how to trace the outline of his foot in the middle of his piece of paper. Then give him the crayons—and let him go to work completing the animal. To give him the idea, show him the pictures above.

A series of these animals makes an attractive wall "zoo" frieze to decorate a child's room.

Indoor Camping with Instant Tents

It takes only a few minutes to set up either of these simple tents—"playhouses" your child can enjoy while you are busy with something else or that can keep him occupied after you have to leave him at home with a baby-sitter.

Card-table Tent

Make this hideout by setting up a card table and then covering it with a blanket or a sheet. Presto!—a pirates' den, a secret cave, a private clubhouse.

Chair Tent

For this tent, you will need:

    2 straight-backed chairs
    8′ of clothesline
    a sheet or blanket

This tent takes a bit more room, but is equally effective in creating your child's own "space."

Place two straight-backed chairs approximately 8′ apart with the backs facing each other. Then tie the ends of the clothesline to the top of each chair and adjust the chairs so that the line is taut.

Finally, hang a blanket or a sheet over the clothesline and anchor the sides that hang onto the floor with some heavy books. The kids can then lift up a flap and crawl inside and out.

A Word About Glue

For projects that require glue, almost any brand will do as long as you remember to ask for glue or paste that is "water-based." Elmer's glue is handy, but you can even make your own flour-and-water paste if you want to.

A bit of extravagance that pays off in saving mess is the purchase of a "glue stick." It looks and works like a chapstick and can be purchased at the dime store or an art store. Some children find a glue stick easier to handle than trying to estimate the right amount of paste they need for sticking things together.

Paper-plate Fish

This amusing fish helps to show children how one shape can be easily transformed into another. Kids love the "surprise ending."

    MATERIALS:
        1 round paper plate
        scissors
        crayon
        glue stick

Help your child cut a triangular wedge from one side of the paper plate.

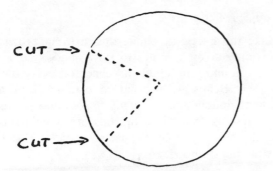

Show him how to use the crayons to draw a large lidless eye, a breathing gill, and protective scales. Then glue the wedge you have cut out to the side of the plate opposite the open mouth of the fish—for a tail!

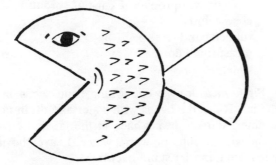

Clothes Puzzle

This puzzle helps children to learn the names of articles of clothing as well as to develop some sense of right and left.

MATERIALS:
- picture magazines or coloring book
- scissors
- glue stick
- lightweight cardboard
- Magic Markers or crayons

Find in a magazine or a child's coloring book a good-sized picture (advertisements are a likely source) of a standing person wearing everyday clothes (for example, man dressed in coat and trousers; woman in blouse and skirt; child in overalls and T-shirt, or raincoat and boots). Glue the picture to a piece of lightweight cardboard and cut out the figure.

On another piece of lightweight cardboard, use a Magic Marker to trace around the outline of the cutout figure. Then cut the figure into puzzle pieces. Each piece should be a recognizable part of an article of clothing (coat sleeve, skirt, shoe, etc.).

Glue the cut-off head of the figure onto the puzzle outline. Then show your child how to fit the other loose puzzle pieces onto the outline to "dress" the figure. The outline will help him to fit the right arm and sleeve onto the right side; the left foot and shoe onto the left side, and so on.

RAPID GARDENER

Watching things grow indoors can be a satisfying shared project for you and your children all year long. Here are a few easy ways to develop that interest—all with guaranteed relatively quick results.

Plant Doctor

Rare is the American home today that is not inhabited by at least one house plant, if not a dozen. Why not make the daily chore of watering and caring for the home jungle something you do with your preschooler? This task is a lot more aesthetic than some other chores you might ask him to help you with (such as taking out the garbage) and is a part of housework he can take pride in.

Planting Narcissus Bulbs

Narcissus bulbs are ideal for young gardeners because they require little effort to plant, a minimum of tending to grow, and are guaranteed to stay in bloom for at least a week. They are fun to plant indoors in the wintertime, and can be started every few weeks to provide continuing flowers.

If you are ambitious, you can plant a bowl of several bulbs, but a child is often satisfied with one.

YOU WILL NEED:
    1 paper cup
    small pebbles or planting soil
    1 paper-white narcissus bulb

Fill the cup with the soil or the pebbles. Set the bulb in the planting material so that the tip is just above the surface. Water thoroughly (if you use pebbles, the water should come up to the level of the pebbles).

To make the bulb grow, it must be placed in a dark cool place for a week (the bottom shelf of a refrigerator or in the basement does nicely). You can explain to your child that this way you are creating a "make-believe" winter for the plant. While the plant is in the dark, its roots will grow. Check every day or so to make sure the soil is moist or that the water is up to the level of the pebbles.

After a week, take the bulb out of the dark and place it in full sunlight. Now the top of the plant will begin to grow, and the green shoots will get taller and taller until buds form and the plant is ready to bloom. You should have flowers within 10 days to 2 weeks after the plant comes out of the dark.

From planting to bloom takes about three weeks. If your child enjoys watching the narcissus grow, you can help him to start a plant every week so that he can always have a flower. If he wants to give narcissus plants for Christmas presents, he should start them about Thanksgiving time.

Bean Sprouts

Like the narcissus bulbs, this growing project takes only a few minutes to start—and is something you and your child can check on every day together. Beans will sprout in containers in a kitchen window and are ready to toss into salads in as few as four days. Sprouts are a delicious crunchy snack just by themselves—and are rich in vitamins B and E.

MATERIALS:
    1 quart-sized glass jar—clean and empty, preferably wide-mouthed
    Mung bean seeds (buy these at a health food store or a Chinese grocery; ¼ cup seeds will produce 4 cups of sprouts)
    cheesecloth
    rubber band
    measuring cup
    water

First, measure ¼ cup Mung bean seeds into the jar. Rinse the beans with water and drain in a strainer. Put the beans back in the jar and cover them with 2 cups of warm water. Leave the jar uncovered and let stand overnight.

The next day, drain the beans in a strainer. They will be swollen to almost double their original size from absorbing the water. Put the beans back in the jar and cover the jar with cheesecloth held in place with a rubber band. Explain to your child that now the beans are ready to grow. They must be kept moist, but not wet.

On the third day, you will see definite signs of growth. Rinse the sprouts by filling the jar with water and turning it upside down. The cheesecloth will act like a strainer. Rinse and drain the sprouts twice a day.

By the fourth or fifth day, the Mung bean sprouts should be 2–3 inches long and ready to eat. Rinse and drain them again and store them in the refrigerator in a plastic bag or covered container. They will keep fresh for a week.

JUST BEFORE BED

Tell Me a Story

If you *are* a natural raconteur, you are miles ahead of most of us. Cultivate whatever germ of this talent you may possess by making up a story for your child each night—or inventing a serial with exciting installments—and you will have a very special bond between you indeed.

Jokes and Riddles

If you are absolutely tongue-tied around a preschooler, try learning some jokes and riddles. You may not be a natural stand-up comedian, but little kids love the kind of silly jokes that will take you back to your own childhood. Your library should have several good joke books in the juvenile section. Until you get there, here are a few elephant jokes to get you started.

How do you know an elephant will stay for a long time when it comes to visit?
Because it brings its trunk.

How can you tell if elephants have been in your refrigerator?
By the footprints in the butter.

Why are elephants so wrinkled?
Did you ever try to iron one?

What time is it when an elephant sits on a fence?
Time to get a new fence.

Why do elephants wear dark sunglasses?
If you had all those jokes told about you, wouldn't you want to hide?

For an encore, try these old chestnuts (they're still new to kids!):

What did one potato chip say to another?
Let's go for a dip.

What did the penny say to the dime?
It would make cents if we went steady.

Why is an old car like a baby?
It has a rattle.

Why was the little shoe so sad?
Its mother was a sneaker and its father was a loafer.

What did the turkey say before it was roasted in the oven?
Boy, am I stuffed!

What did the big flower say to the little flower?
Hi, Bud!

Record Lullaby

There are very few things that I would suggest you buy for a preschooler, but if you wanted to make a worthwhile investment that would last several years, I would put a small portable record player that he can operate himself at the top of the list. Very often you can find an inexpensive one at a neighborhood garage sale.

My own children amused themselves for hours when they were small playing their own records during the early morning, at naptime, during quiet times in their rooms, and, of course, just before bed. You can even put a small portable radio in a child's room— if he can be trusted to keep it on stations that don't drive you bananas!

CHAPTER THREE

Easy Does It Sequel: Just Once a Week

Preview:

MONDAY: HOBBIES AND HOMEWORK

TUESDAY: IT'S SO NICE TO HAVE A CHILD AROUND THE HOUSE

WEDNESDAY: BIG DINNER NIGHTS

THURSDAY: MYSTERY VOYAGES

FRIDAY: FROM SUPERMARKET TO NUTS

SATURDAY: FANATIC FANS

SUNDAY: LET'S BE OLD-FASHIONED

IF A DAILY ROUTINE IS IMPOSSIBLE FOR YOU, WHY not try concentrating your dose of "quality time" in a once-a-week "special treat"? Particularly if you have a large family, setting aside individual time for each child can mean a lot to both of you. If you are a weekend parent, a Sunday special may be the only solution. If you are an everyday frazzled parent—trying to run a house, a family, and a job—making a weekly appointment on your calendar may be the most practical way to fit everything in.

Some grown-ups don't seem to have any trouble scheduling a weekly appointment at the hairdresser or a weekly tennis game; but when it comes to making a date with their kids, they think that sounds artificial. I think it's just a way of reminding your children that they are important. Even if your only commitment is a promise to take them to the Thursday afternoon soccer practice and watch them play, knowing they can count on you for that one thing—come hell or high water—goes a long way toward letting them know that you value the time spent with them.

As you try to cram everything into your weekly calendar, ask yourself, what are your priorities with your kids? Finding time for them shouldn't be a duty just because it's so easy to let other worthwhile things—the P.T.A., lunch with a friend, catching up on mending, taking a course

—erode the kids' time away. With a little foresight, you can work your children into more of your ordinary routines than you may have realized. Taking your preschooler along while you do your Saturday morning errands may give you some unexpected minutes to talk while you are in the car or on the bus. A friend of mine triggered real enthusiasm for tennis in her four-year-old by letting him be the "ball boy" at her weekly tennis game. And some chores you consider boring can result in a kind of "pragmatic education" in how people take care of themselves: My kids, for instance, were fascinated when a shoe-repair man took them in the back of the store and showed them how he attached new heels and polished scuffed toes with a buffer. In other words, just making room for kids at times when there are things you have to do or like to do anyway can help to keep them from feeling shortchanged by your complicated life. They may even begin to understand some of all the other demands on your time!

Listed below are several ideas from other busy parents of activities they have found work with their kids—even only once a week. The suggestions for each day are interchangeable, of course, but may start you thinking about what would fit into your routine—without cramping your style.

MONDAY: HOBBIES AND HOMEWORK

Most children don't have real homework assignments until they are well into grade school. But if your child goes to nursery school or kindergarten, he may occasionally be asked to bring in something from home—perhaps materials for a class project (such as old socks for hand puppets), or money for a field trip. When this happens, you are likely to be faced with two extremes: the child who insists he HAS TO have so-and-so by tomorrow morning ("THE TEACHER SAID" may mean the teacher only mentioned so-and-so in passing), or the child who doesn't remember until just before he leaves the house in the morning—if he remembers at all—that he is supposed to take something to school.

To avoid last-minute tears and confusion, I think it's a good idea early in the year to check

in with your child's teacher. Ask if your child will be expected to produce something from home now and then, and how those responsibilities will be communicated—verbally to the class or by a note to you. Once you have an idea of how the teacher operates, then you can do your part in helping your child to follow through at home. Especially if you are a working mother or father, with a zillion other things on your mind, some kind of continuing dialogue with your child's teacher is a practical necessity. It's too easy for busy parents to delegate too much to a school—and then not be satisfied with the results.

When kids do start bringing papers and drawings home from school, you will probably want to post them in a conspicuous place—such as on the refrigerator door or a family bulletin board. Children love the encouragement. They are just as sensitive as adults to criticism, however, so do beware of displaying any work that might give other kids in the family an excuse to tease—messy handwriting, for example. Some families I know sidestep this unnecessary competitiveness by putting up only the best papers of the week.

Everybody has a different theory as to how much parents should participate when real homework does begin. Perhaps I have known too many overzealous parents who end up doing the work themselves—drawing the maps, solving the math problems, memorizing the spelling lists—but my philosophy is simple: Let the children do as much as they can on their own; be available to help when they are stuck.

Whatever approach you do take, I think most study experts agree that establishing a regular time for homework is fundamental in developing self-discipline. Try to work out with your child a study time that you can both live with—after school, after dinner, whatever works best. Even if you can be available at that time only once a week, you'll be helping your child form solid study habits. And often the assignments young children bring home are as much concerned with instilling good study habits as they are with mastering content.

Before homework crowds the agenda, however, or on that evening when older kids have no assignments, why not take advantage of that set-aside time to start an ongoing project together. Almost any hobby you enjoy—photography, woodworking, pottery—a preschooler would find fascinating. Even simpler are the suggestions that follow.

Start a Collection

Some children are born hoarders and collectors from the time they first pick up a pretty stone in the back yard and within days have a rock pile in their bedrooms. Others simply pass through a baseball card or stamp or doll collecting phase. Whenever you spot this urge in any form, it's a good idea to try to channel the natural acquisitiveness of little kids—and perhaps to lay the foundation for a lifetime hobby.

Remember, it takes only two items to start a collection. Very small children can look for natu-

"I'M NOT A PACK RAT! I'M A CONNOISSEUR!"

ral things—leaves, rocks, shells. You can help in the identifying, cataloguing, and displaying of these treasures (Chapters Eight and Nine both contain suggestions). You might have to do a little research in the library, but the results are usually worth it. "My collection" is one of the things that makes a child feel unique.

As children grow older, almost anything under the sun—from model building to a museum trip to a postcard—can be the inspiration for a frenzy of hoarding. Stickers, decals, and pennants are popular in my neighborhood right now, but perennial favorites include:

stamps (post office has good starter sets)
foreign money
T-shirts
buttons (both the clothes kind and the pin-
   on slogans)
posters
hats
toy soldiers
autographs
matchbooks
mugs
masks and disguises
comic books
records

One child I know even collects ball-point pens, each advertising a different company name.

If you're a collector yourself, it may be second nature to you to try to start your child in a similar direction. But more important than what a child collects, I think, is the respect you give his intention.

I was somewhat taken aback when at age ten

my daughter began saving beer cans. But the same things happened to her that might have had she been collecting antique dolls. Friends and relatives heard about her interest—and brought her samples from all over the world. Discussing her collection with them and other can aficionados gave her something new to talk about—and led to new friendships. Certainly, her display of cans made her room unique. And through organizing her collection, she saw some advantages of being more organized in other aspects of her life. It may be just a phase she's going through, but in tolerating her eccentricities, I think I've learned to appreciate some of her individuality that I might have overlooked.

As with kids' homework, however, one word of warning about going overboard on collections. If grown-ups get too involved, it's too easy for them to concentrate on building the perfect collection instead of letting the child develop his own interest at his own rate. There's no more classic example of parent takeover than the elaborate electric train set with switches a preschooler can't work and a model village he couldn't care less about. Kids' enthusiasm for a collection is what motivates their involvement—not a beautiful display or the accumulation of value. Ultimately, it's their interest that enhances their capacity for self-amusement and entertainment.

"Someday Scrapbooks"

I daresay there is hardly a family in the United States that does not have a drawer full of unmounted photographs or boxes of memorabilia in the attic waiting to be preserved in a scrapbook—someday. For an ongoing one-night-a-week family project, let the children help you organize those irreplaceable bits of history into family albums.

Photo albums are usually the most fun. Kids love to sift through pictures of themselves as babies, gawk at pictures of you and other relatives in days gone by, recite the adventures of the last vacation. Particularly for those of us who move frequently or who now live far away from our roots, old photos can impart a sense of Family (with a capital F) that transplanted kids so often find missing. Now that diary writers are the exception rather than the rule, photographs tend to be the best way we have of continuing a family

record. I can't guarantee this project will empty that drawer, however. Every time the kids and I work on bringing our family album up to date, I find I'm inspired to haul out my camera and shoot the next chapter!

Individual scrapbooks for each child are priceless momentoes—if you can keep them going. Many young mothers keep a "baby book" dutifully during the child's first year—recording each inch, pound, and gurgle—then become too bogged down to continue. Try saving just a few things from each year—a preschool drawing, a funny remark written down, a birthday card. These can go a long way toward creating a unique childhood history. Once a month or so, you might sit down with your child and work on a scrapbook that keeps an ongoing record of who he is.

For a less elaborate project, try one of these *one-night stands:*

1. Make a "Me" book (Chapter One)
2. Construct a "Touch Me" book (Chapter Nine)
3. Cut out pictures from magazines for a "Crazy Notebook" (Chapter Five)
4. Think up with your child your own theme for cutting and pasting pictures: "Places I'd Like to Go" (old *National Geographics* are a gold mine); "People I'd Like to Meet" (try news magazines); sports heroes; cars; animals—you name it, the possibilities are endless. One mother I know had good luck with a just-beginning-to-talk child by cutting out pictures he simply pointed to and pasting them into a scrapbook for a "First Word" book.

Year Boxes

A year box is a special kind of "scrapbook" —sort of like a tiny time capsule. Suppose you could open up a box for every year of your life. What might you find inside? Some families keep year boxes—instead of scrapbooks—for each child and present them to the subject on their eighteenth or twenty-first birthdays. You don't need big boxes—shoe boxes or even smaller ones will do—to keep small tokens of sentiment: a lock of hair from a first haircut, a baby shoe, a favorite toy, a cub scout necktie, a braces retainer. To mark each year, you might include political buttons, bumper stickers, newspaper headlines, coins, or calendars. The result is both amusing and unique.

Gift Wrapping

While you are thinking about making presents, you might also start collecting materials for unusual gift wrapping. Containers from your recycle box (see Chapter Four) will be useful: egg cartons, milk cartons, coffee cans—can all be disguised with glued-on construction paper or poster paints to look like fancy packages. An oatmeal box, for example, makes a dandy drum hiding who knows what surprise inside.

A celebrity journalist I know always wraps his gifts to friends in copies of his newspaper column. I don't know why more people don't do the same. Newspaper or comic papers with a bright ribbon can wrap a gay package. In fact, leftover paper of almost any kind—wallpaper, shelf paper bright paper bags—can dress up the most humble gift. A preschooler could even use one of his drawings to wrap up a package.

Paper bags are especially useful for containing gifts with peculiar shapes. Magic Markers can do wonders to embellish a plain old brown grocery bag. Place the gift inside and tie the top with yarn. For extra dash, fringe the top of the bag with your scissors.

Aluminum foil can literally be pressed into service when you are in a pinch. A bit expensive, but it gives glitter, particularly to small gifts.

Something for Everyone on Your List

In the chapters that follow, you'll find many suggestions for projects that are suitable for gifts. Children catch on quickly to the idea that almost anything they can make at home is not only inexpensive, but also very personal—a gift of themselves. A collage, for example (Chapter Eight), is guaranteed to please. Even a two-year-old (you can do the pasting if you have to) can assemble something that looks good. Some other ideas:

FOR GRANDPARENTS:
    salt-dough plaque of hand or foot (Chapter One)
    pressed-leaf book cover (Chapter Nine)
FOR MOTHER:
    paper-tube flower holder (Chapter Four)
    potholder rack (Chapter Four)
FOR FATHER:
    pencil holder (Chapter Four)
    mobile (Chapter Ten)
    shell-and-stone paperweight (Chapter Eight)
FOR SISTER OR BROTHER:
    clothespin dolls and soldiers (Chapter Five)
    bathtub boats (Chapter One and Chapter Five)
    spool railway engine and train (Chapter Five)
    kites (Chapter Six)
FOR FRIEND:
    saltbox bank (Chapter Two)
    toy box (Chapter Four)
FOR TEACHER:
    paper tulips (Chapter Four)
    narcissus bulbs (Chapter Two)
FOR RELATIVE:
    potholder rack (Chapter Four)
    rock bookends (Chapter Six)
FOR NEIGHBOR:
    egg-carton treasure chest (Chapter Four)
    pumpkin seeds (Chapter Six)

TUESDAY: IT'S SO NICE TO HAVE A CHILD AROUND THE HOUSE

I must confess I have mixed feelings about a common parental precept: that everybody must have a chore. Jenny, my twelve-year-old, happens to go to school from seven forty-five in the morning to five o'clock in the afternoon. I would like to be one of those mothers who says proudly, "Oh, yes, she certainly has her jobs around the house."

But if I insist she have a regular list of chores, she literally won't have time to do anything else. When she comes home at five, she's already had her workday. She's probably got homework that will keep her busy until she goes to bed. If she had a chore routine, too, she would have no time for play at all. And I suspect we would have a daily hassle over what she had not had time to do.

What works for me has been a practical compromise. Jenny is expected to take care of her room. Period. But when I am really pushed and need help—with dog walking, table setting, picking up yard litter, whatever—I expect her to pitch in without complaint. I find that I get far less grumbling when I save my requests for pressured times. When Jenny can see that helping is a necessity, not busy work, she understands that those chores make sense.

Some sort of household responsibility, whether it's regularly scheduled or not, does, I think, give kids a sense of belonging and of permanence. Just being trusted to do their part lets them know their contribution is valued. But admit to yourself that what you may think is perfectly reasonable is bound to meet with some resistance. No matter what kinds of chores you assign your kids,

I can guarantee you'll have more success than frustration if you keep them simple.

Housework

Tiny children like to follow you around when you're cleaning house. They probably can't help much, but you can let them participate. Try a dustcloth with a preschooler. Keep him away from breakables and let him practice on a big piece of furniture—such as a coffee table. Or show him how to empty wastebaskets. Collecting baskets one at a time from rooms of the house and bringing them to a central place to empty will keep him busy and make him feel useful.

Let's be honest, though. Emptying the garbage is the pits. Even grown-ups hate it. Rather than assigning this job to the littlest kid on the totem pole, why not rotate it in the family? Be a good sport and take your turn, too.

You'll probably have the most success with asking the children to take care of their own rooms simply because they have to live with the results. Some parents just close the doors to kids' rooms. Others require a minimum of order: a made bed, clean clothes put away, dirty clothes deposited in the laundry hamper. (Even a preschooler can make a bed with the new pull-up coverlets.) If you are a compulsive neatnik, try to remember that it took years for you to become that way. Insisting on a white-glove inspection and a spotless room can add only needless tension.

If you can allow a child to live as he likes in his own room, then I think you can enforce a stricter neatness code in the common areas of the house where everyone has an obligation to respect the rights of others. That can mean no shoes abandoned in the living room, no food left out in the kitchen, no personal "junk" adorning the stairs. It can also mean that your child's room may look more like a Fibber McGee walk-in closet than the decorator's model room you had envisioned, but be practical—and patient.

Pets

IF you decide to have a family pet—and no matter how small the pet, it's still a big IF, I suggest you do some background research. It's well worth your time and money to visit a few pet stores and buy a pamphlet or two to find out what's involved in caring for the creature of your choice. Tiny white mice and gerbils, for example, look easy to handle, but are remarkably clever at escaping from their cages and losing themselves in the crannies of your house. That adorable hamster will bite if the kids tease him too much. Sturdy as he appears, the amiable guinea pig tends to get sick.

Then consider the ongoing expense of your pet's life-style. He may be a bargain in the store, but you will probably need a cage, bedding, toys, and, of course food. If the pet becomes ill, there may be veterinarian bills. And unless you have a reliable volunteer pet-sitter, every time the family plans a vacation, you will have to figure in the cost of pet care while you are away.

Finally, no matter what your children promise in the pet store, remember that you will end up taking care of the animal. Goldfish and guppies sound simple, but eventually someone has to clean the algae out of the tank. Finches sing sweetly and breed easily, but scatter seed and mess up their cages. And it goes without saying that cats scratch furniture and dogs stain rugs.

Despite the discouraging drawbacks, if you do opt to become the parent of a pet, then rest assured that there's probably nothing that will give your child more hours of company and pleasure. Under your guidance, little ones can help with the care and feeding of goldfish, gerbils, and guinea pigs and enjoy the responsibility of taking care of a live creature. A dog or a cat is a much bigger proposition, but in the long run provides a more rewarding relationship. Just be realistic in recognizing that any pet is a family pet, not a child's property. If you can be counted on to do your share of the work, then Rover and Kitty are well worth adopting. The love of a pet is the nicest, most undemanding relationship any child can have.

Gardening

Although it's hard for small children to become involved in your Harry Homeowner projects around the house, gardening is something they can enjoy in a big way. Remember one ground rule, however: If you want kids to like gardening, you will have better luck if you miniaturize. Most children think apple trees are a nifty idea, for example, but have no interest in pruning, fertilizing, or spraying the trees. Because the maintenance of a big garden is so overwhelming, an ideal solution is to give each child a tiny space of his own to till.

If you don't have a big back yard, try a pot garden (Chapter Six). In either case, help your

child to pick out something special and easy he would like to grow. Seed catalogues and garden stores usually feature selections aimed at kids. Pumpkins and zucchini offer big results with little attention. And cherry tomatoes and sugar snap peas are practically no fail; children can eat both right off the vine. Your child can have as much fun and success with only two bountiful plants as he could with a whole patch.

From a small garden a child can also learn a great deal about ecology. To feed his plants, you can show him how to make a miniature compost heap (Chapter Six). If you don't have space in your back yard for compost, let him make some in a coffee can. It doesn't take long to collect grass clippings, leaves, egg shells, etc. in a can. Then he will have his own natural fertilizer to put around the two or three plants in his garden.

WEDNESDAY: BIG DINNER NIGHTS

In busy families where both parents work and there are children of different ages on different schedules, sitting down together around the dinner table often seems like an impossible dream. One doctor's family I know tackled the problem head-on by deciding to make a weekly common family meal a treat, rather than a chore.

After a family discussion, everyone agreed that Wednesday night was the one time they would schedule an evening meal together at 7:30—a "big dinner"—no matter what. On those days, the doctor whose routine usually kept him at the office until after eight, rearranged his day so that he could be home by 6:30. His wife, a social worker, did the same. Even though the kids had to snack to stave off hunger, everyone sat down to a leisurely meal at 7:30. Sometimes the food was simple, sometimes elaborate. Almost always, someone's favorite dish was a highlight. If there was an occasion to celebrate, everyone dressed up. But what the doctor's children remember are the long, comfortable conversations in which everyone joined. More important than the meal was the time that their parents had set aside to be with them—time for the family to feel like a family. It may sound artificial, but to both those children and parents, "big dinner" nights became a tradition to look forward to.

At our house we have a simpler routine, but it has also gradually become a family ritual. I save Sunday nights to have supper with the children. In winter, we sit by the fire and have sourdough bread and soup. In summer we are usually outdoors—with a picnic. Sometimes the children invite friends, but we enjoy the evening most when there are just us.

Before you go overboard in inventing your own "big dinner" (or "tiny dinner") tradition, however, be sure your children are old enough to appreciate the time you are giving up for them. A weekend evening means nothing to a year-old child and a great deal to kids whose parents work all day and who are in school or day care themselves. Children three or under are apt to get so tired and cranky when they are kept up and meals are delayed that it's much simpler to let them eat earlier and spend some other kind of time with them when you get home. Companionship is the best feast of all.

Special Events

If you simply cannot arrange a regular weekly family dinner, compromise by an occasional celebration. In Chapter Ten you will find suggestions for making almost any day of the year a special event. Let the kids help you in setting the table, even in making decorations. A birthday is always a grand excuse for a family party, but an "unbirthday" can be just as much fun—if only because you can have one anytime.

THURSDAY: MYSTERY VOYAGES

Most kids I know instinctively loathe shopping. Can't you recall being dragged along (or so you thought) on excursions you found incredibly boring? Remember that the attention span of small children is amazingly short. When you take them with you on a round of errands, try to break up the routine with a stop they might enjoy. The promise of a surprise side trip—a "mystery voyage"—can relieve the tedium by giving you both something to anticipate.

World Tours in a Market

Any ethnic grocery store can be fascinating to children, especially one where they can watch foods being prepared. For instance, my kids love to go to the Italian market in Baltimore. If I have to take them with me to the supermarket, I sometimes plan a visit to the Italian market as part of the over-all trip. Everything smells so good, and there are so many intriguing foods to look at and to eat: pasta being cut and dried, big hunks of cheese, meatball subs, rum cakes, even barrels of snails. On really busy days we often pick out our supper at the carry-out counter and take it home to eat. (Kids are fickle about strange food, but they will often try something different just because it looks different.)

Along with the exotic, in any foreign specialty food store kids are bound to find something familiar. Look for fortune cookies in a Chinese grocery (great to tuck into lunch boxes), croissants at a French bakery (try them for unusual sandwiches), pita bread and yogurt at a Middle Eastern shop. When you feel adventuresome, introduce the kids to honeyed baklava and feta cheese at a Greek deli or liverwurst at a German butcher. You might point out, too, that many foreign snacks have rapidly become adopted as American fast foods: Chinese egg rolls, Italian pizza, Mexican tacos—all originally concocted by busy working people who had to eat on the run. If you live in a large city, you may very well have an international delicatessen or open-air market housing all kinds of goodies from other cultures under one roof.

Making a point of becoming acquainted with different kinds of cheese and bread, a staple meal in many European countries, can literally give your children a taste of what life is like across the Atlantic. Cheese shops rarely refuse requests for sample slivers. Your kids might like the flavor of brie (France), blue (Denmark), gruyere (Switzerland), cheddar (England), Jarlsberg (Norway), bel paese or mozzarella (Italy), edam or gouda (Netherlands). Except for Danish blue most of these cheeses are mild tasting.

With the cheese, let your child experiment with nibbles of French or Italian bread, Swedish braided loaves, German pumpernickel or rye—even Danish pastries. At some bakeries, kids can watch bread being baked, then select something they'd like to take home to eat.

Hardware Hits

You don't have to be a Mr. Fixit type to discover that your neighborhood hardware store is a gold mine of inexpensive items easily adapted to kids' toys and projects.

For example, for less than a dollar, you can buy one yard of contact paper to cover a shoe box at home. *Voilà*—an instant treasure chest. Add bright tape for trim if you like.

For less than five dollars, you can smartly outfit a back-yard sandbox with:

> wood spoons (also great for drumsticks)
> plastic measuring spoons and cups (also helpful for playing house)
> metal strainers and sifters
> plastic paint buckets (also for toting and storing small toys)

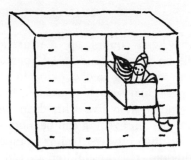

(You will find directions for an easy homemade sandbox in Chapter Six.)

Other favorite finds for kids are:

A FLASHLIGHT:
> fun to flash the light
> practical to keep on a bedside table
> easy to take apart and see how it works

A MULTI-DRAWERED NAIL OR SCREW CHEST:
> this kind of box (in all sizes—usually metal or plastic with tiny clear plastic drawers) is intriguing as a toy in itself. Taking the drawers out and fitting them back in entertains and challenges preschoolers much as a block puzzle does. The drawers are just right for storing the small items small hands collect—stones, toy soldiers, shoelaces, string, etc. Older children can use the box as a desk organizer to file away stamps, paper clips, thumbtacks, etc.

TOOLS:
> toy tool chests, except for the very youngest children, are less fun than the real thing. Begin your collection with:
>> large nuts and bolts: fun to feel, to examine the shape of, to play with (like buttons)
>> a small hammer
>> a small screwdriver that will twist big screws (make sure handles on both hammer and screwdriver are easily held by small hands)
>> a box of nails
>> a piece of pegboard and hooks for hanging the tools (optional)

You don't have to buy the pegboard, but if you do, getting it ready for storing the tools is a good follow-up project to the hardware store trip. Lay the pegboard on a table or the floor and let your child arrange the tools on the board. Show him how to use a Magic Marker to trace around each tool to leave an outline. (If the Marker doesn't show up clearly on the board, you may want to go over the outline with paint.) Hang up the board, insert the pegs, and your child can have fun organizing his new equipment by matching the tools to their outlined shapes.

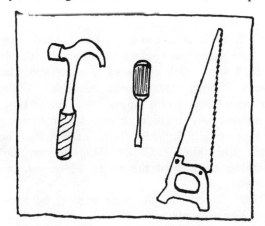

To practice using tools, stop by your local lumberyard and ask for some scraps. Under your supervision, a preschooler can construct some unrecognizable but satisfying objects—just by nailing a few pieces of wood together.

FRIDAY: FROM SUPERMARKET TO NUTS

With the weekend coming up, a relaxed Friday night might be a good time to let your children share in the shopping and cooking for an easy meal. In particular, single parents whose kids visit them rather than live with them regularly, tell me that such an evening can be more fun and less artificial than always feeling compelled to take the kids out. If your children are old enough to plan a menu and to shop within a budget (probably six or seven), you'll also be teaching them some valuable lessons in nutrition and economics. Let them buy anything, but make clear they must eat their purchases. That's the deal.

Red, Yellow, and Green

Be prepared for a wild menu when you first turn over the shopping cart to a youngster. He's apt to decide that potato chips, french fried potatoes, ice cream, and cookies would make a dandy dinner. I don't think you need to worry about an occasional crazy meal; even "sensible" adults who know better go on binges from time to time. But an easy way to guide his selection from being too nutritionally lopsided is to suggest that he choose something red, something yellow, and something green (not the boxes, of course, but the food).

These colors almost guarantee a balanced menu. For example:

Red	Yellow	Green
most raw meat	corn	peas
tomatoes	cheese	beans—limas
apples	summer squash	and snap
grapes	wax beans	salad leaves
red onions	pineapple	grapes
	bananas	broccoli
		asparagus

Shopping by colors also creates a pretty plate. You can add others: For orange, try carrots and oranges. For purple, eggplant and grapes. For white, rice, potatoes, bread, and milk.

Pocketbook Issues

Whatever shopping you do for your evening together, experiment with letting your child handle the money. Depending on your budget, give him five or ten dollars and let him shop for both of you. If he spends too much, he'll have to put something back on the shelf and rethink his choices. That's life . . .

Four Easy Menus

1. Baked Potato Buffet

Seasoned only with butter, salt, and pepper, a single baked potato is a hot nutritious meal by itself. Bake one for each child (1 hour at 350° F.), split it on his plate, and top with one or more of the following. (Be sure to invent your own concoctions, as this is a great way to stretch or use up leftovers. Remember that anything kids like on a pizza, they will love on a baked potato.)

crumbled bacon	tuna fish salad
chopped tomato	cooked hamburger
sliced hard-boiled egg	(instant shepherd's
melted cheese	pie)
cottage cheese	sliced ham, chicken,
chopped onions	pot roast—any
mixed vegetables	leftover meat
(peas and carrots,	
for example)	

2. Vegetable Soup and Open-"face" Peanut-butter Sandwiches

Open up a can of one of the many excellent vegetable soups available and spend your energy helping your child create these amusing edible "faces" on single slices of bread.

MATERIALS:

peanut butter, cheese, plain butter, or any kind of smooth spread

peanuts, raisins, sliced maraschino cherries, bananas, etc., for eyes, noses, and mouths

> grated cabbage, lettuce leaves, shredded carrots, coconut, and parsley for hair and beards
> sliced bread

After your child has spread peanut butter on a slice of bread, let him use whatever trimmings you can find in the refrigerator or cupboard to make a funny face. If you are fixing a meal for a group of kids, you might want to use different kinds of bread—rye, whole wheat, or pumpernickel—as well as good old standby white—for a variety of complexions.

To fancy up the sandwiches, cut the bread into shapes beforehand with a round glass, a knife, or a cookie cutter. Kids also enjoy making these for their own parties—birthday or rainy day "unbirthday."

3. Cheese Fondue

A fondue is a dish of melted food, in this case, a pot of a melted cheese mixture into which everyone dips cubes of bread. The notion of eating from a common pot is novel to most children, and therefore, entertaining in itself. Special fondue equipment—a pot with its own burner to put on a table and long-handled forks—is useful, but not necessary. You can improvise with any double-boiler top, regular forks, and even fingers if the bread chunks are big enough.

Kids might like to know that fondue is the French word for "melted," and that the dish originated centuries ago in the French-speaking part of Switzerland. Add a salad and/or fruit for a good simple repast, especially on a cold night. Our version substitutes milk for the traditional white wine, but the basic proportions of cheese to liquid are standard in most fondue recipes.

INGREDIENTS:
> 2 cups low-fat milk (or 2 cups white wine or 2 cups beer)
> 1 pound Swiss cheese—grated
> 3 tablespoons flour
> freshly ground pepper ⎫ omit if kids
> dash of nutmeg ⎭ like it plainer
> cubes of bread (at least 1 inch; chunks of French bread are even better)

Heat the liquid slowly in the top of a double boiler to a simmer. Dredge the grated cheese with the flour, and drop by handfuls into the liquid. Stir slowly with a wood spoon until the mixture is bubbling. Add the seasonings and remove from the stove.

Place the fondue pot (or double boiler) and the bread chunks in the middle of the table. Everyone takes turns dipping the bread into the cheese. Be sure each child has a plate to put his bread and cheese on in case the mixture is too hot.

4. Eggs in a Nest

Kids who like eggs might be persuaded to develop an affinity for spinach, too, with this easy one-dish meal. Arrange cooked spinach on a plate so that it serves as a "nest" for a hard-boiled or poached egg. Restaurants call this combination "Eggs Florentine" when they accompany the dish with a topping of Hollandaise sauce.

Veggie Ventures

Raw vegetables can add vitamins and color to any meal, and, in fact, some children actually prefer vegetables uncooked. They are also ideal low-calorie snacks for both grown-ups and kids. You can make vegetables more interesting to nibble by showing the kids how to construct edible flowers, faces, and alphabet letters.

For all three, you will need a selection of washed and scrubbed vegetables:

SLICES OF:
> onion (red and white)
> cucumber
> zucchini
> tomato

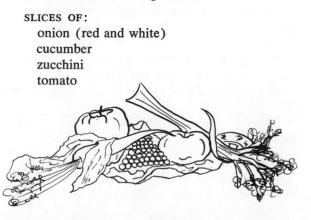

TWO-INCH STICKS OF:
  celery
  carrots
  spring onions
  green pepper
  green beans
  broccoli
  cauliflower
WHOLE:
  radishes
  mushroom caps
SPRIGS OF:
  parsley

PLATE FOR EACH CHILD (use paper, if you have them handy)

Veggie Faces

The plate is the "face." Kids use veggies to suggest features. Try cucumber slices for eyes, a whole radish for a nose, mushroom caps for ears, a carrot stick for a mouth. Sprigs of parsley make wonderful green hair.

Veggie Flowers

Use a round vegetable slice for the flower center, vegetable sticks for petals and stems. Try a tomato center with petals of alternating green pepper and carrots. Green beans make a suitable stem, and parsley sprigs can suggest leaves.

Veggie Alphabet

Give each child a few vegetable sticks and round slices and ask him what letters he can think of to make with them. An "O" from an onion ring should get him going if he seems stumped. Then show him how to make a letter with three of the sticks ("A" or "N", for example). Before tackling the entire alphabet, why not pique his interest by showing him how to make the letters that spell his name? If you're on a no-sweet kick, you can also play a word game with vegetable sticks. Show him how to construct letters that spell "cake" or "candy." He can then eat all of the vegetable "cake" or "candy" his little heart desires.

Dessert Orgy

Why not let your kids splurge on sweets once in a while? They will be less likely to sneak forbidden foods if you admit you've got a sweet tooth, too, and indulge together. Small children can assist in the preparation of the three desserts that follow. Each also is a wonderful mini-meal in itself (I belong to the school that thinks desserts on top of a meal are too much, anyway).

Baked Apples

So simple, so yummy. Wash and core one apple for each person. Peel away the skin only from the top—about ¼ of the way down the fruit. Put the apples in a baking dish. Fill each cored center with a tablespoon of brown or white sugar. Add one tablespoon of water for each apple to the bottom of the dish. Bake at 350° F. until easily pierced with a fork—about 1 hour.

You can do the same with fresh firm pears or peaches. Watch the cooking time, however. Depending on the variety, pears take from 1–3 hours. Peaches will bake in about 20 minutes. They turn out nicely when halved and pitted before being placed in the baking dish.

Ice-cream Snowman

Two round scoops of any kind of ice cream (obviously, vanilla looks most like snow) will make a jolly snowman.

MATERIALS:
  ice cream
  grated coconut (optional)
  raisins
  sticks of candy or licorice
  paper plates
  toothpicks

If you can plan ahead, scoop the snowballs with a round ice-cream scoop ahead of time and place them on a tray in the refrigerator freezer to harden. They will be much easier to work with, and won't melt while the kids are constructing their men.

When ready to make the snowmen, give each child 2 snowballs on a paper plate. On each plate also dole out a few tablespoons of coconut, several raisins, 2 short (2″–3″) sticks of candy or licorice, and 3 or 4 toothpicks.

Show the kids how to roll the snowballs in the coconut to create a "flaky" effect. Then help them use the toothpicks to attach one ball on top of the other to look like a miniature snowman. The raisins are for eyes, nose, buttons. The candy sticks can be gently pressed into each side of the top ball for arms.

Chocolate-bar Fondue

For chocoholics, the sensation of dipping fresh fruit into hot melted chocolate is unbeatable. This is a rich dish, so warn the kids not to overdo. As with cheese fondue, everybody dips into a common pot.

MATERIALS:

    1 pound of chocolate (sweet or semi-sweet)
    ¾ cup light cream
    1 teaspoon vanilla extract
    fresh fruit for dunking: strawberries, chunks of banana, drained pineapple, orange sections, slices of apple

Chop up the chocolate yourself or let the kids break it into small pieces. Put the chocolate into the top of a double-boiler, add the cream, and warm over low heat. Stir the mixture until it is melted and smooth. Remove the pot from the stove and let the kids gather round and start dipping for an unforgettable treat.

Although fruit is traditionally dunked in chocolate fondue, equally delicious dippers are pretzels, zwieback, and saltines.

SATURDAY: FANATIC FANS

When the weekend rolls around, you may want to plan an outing with one or all of your children. Here are some simple, inexpensive suggestions.

Pick a Team

If your family is sports-minded, why settle for watching professional teams on television? Look in the newspapers for the schedules of high school or college teams in your area. Many of these events are free. Little kids will enjoy the color of the contest, especially if they can feel some personal attachment by following the progress of a hometown team. The younger the competing athletes, the better. Best of all is watching an older brother or sister who is on a team.

SUNDAY: LET'S BE OLD-FASHIONED

Sunday is probably the most flexible day of the week, allowing time for some low-key hours together. Perhaps your routine includes church and Sunday school. If yours is an exercising family, you may plan jogging, biking, hiking, or even skiing. Maybe you just sit around the living room and read the newspapers. In making time for the children, remind yourself that it's the repetition of something you do together, not the novelty, that kids remember and value. The suggested activities that follow may sound simple, but they have been rituals in family life for decades.

Perceptive Promenade

A leisurely walk is a time to talk and a time to look. Preoccupied grown-ups are often surprised to realize that their kids have much sharper powers of observation than they do. Take advantage of kids' love of looking for something special as you stroll. Ask who can spot the smallest red thing? The biggest yellow thing? Who can find a smooth stick? A polished stone? Or, give each child a plastic bag and suggest he pick up litter. If you have lots to talk about, forget the games and enjoy the conversation.

Picnic in the Park

For a variation on the back-yard barbecue, pack up the Sunday papers, the kids, and a delicious lunch—and head for your favorite park. City families have always gravitated to parks on weekends, but it seldom occurs to us in suburbia to read the Sunday papers anywhere but at home. While the children inspect the playground equip-

ment (nearly every park has some) or play with toys they've brought along, you can read and snooze. This is a great occasion for people-watching, perhaps the most fun of the afternoon.

Sunday Dress-up: The Old Suitcase Trick

Children do love to dress up in costumes. But sometimes they can be obstinate about abandoning their favorite play clothes to "dress up" as their parents suggest for certain occasions. I generally believe that fights over clothes are one of those hassles that can be eliminated from an already overscheduled day. If you shop carefully, you can buy children's clothing that will suit almost any purpose without having to have special school clothes or special dress-up clothes. But every once in a while an occasion does arise when you want your child to wear something in particular and he absolutely refuses to go out of the house in *anything* but his battered cowboy suit.

A good friend of mine came up with what I consider an extremely practical solution. "I understand how you feel," she said to her protesting little boy, "but this is one time when it means a lot to me to have you wear over to your grandmother's house the corduroy pants she gave you for Christmas. So I'll tell you what. Let's make a compromise." She went to her closet and pulled out a tiny overnight case and showed it to her little boy. "You can put the cowboy suit in this little suitcase," she said, "and take it with you, and carry it around all day. That way you'll know where it is, I'll be happy with how you look, and your grandmother will be pleased that you are wearing her corduroys. And no one will know what is in the little suitcase except you. That can be your own secret." The child was so intrigued with the idea of carrying around a secret in a suitcase that he took off the cowboy suit and packed it up right away. He was also reassured that he would not have to leave behind something that gave him the security he felt he needed —in this case it was a cowboy suit, but it could easily have been a blanket, a toy, or some other object that an adult might consider trivial, but a child regards as crucial.

CHAPTER FOUR

Kitchen Toyshop: Recipes for Recycling

Preview:

MAGNIFICENT MILK CARTONS

SENSATIONAL CEREAL BOXES

ELEGANT EGG CARTONS

TERRIFIC PAPER-TOWEL TUBES

BEAUTIFUL BROWN BAGS

CLEVER TIN CANS

INCREDIBLE CONTAINERS

AMAZING ALUMINUM TINS

GORGEOUS GROCERY BOXES

THE NEXT TIME THE CHILDREN BADGER YOU with whines of boredom, march right into the kitchen and show them how to "cook" up a new toy with leftovers—not with uneaten food, but with containers you might otherwise throw away.

For example, small children love to play with toys that make noise. One Saturday afternoon my kids and I found we could easily transform several discarded boxes and bottles into musical instruments—into what I like to call a "Recycle Rhythm Band." Here's what we concocted:

An empty salt container is perfect for filling with rice, unpopped popcorn, stones, and/or dried pasta to make a Mexican *maraca*.

If you want to fancy up the maraca, cover the box with glued-on construction paper, draw birds and flowers on the paper. Then, shake, rattle, and roll!

An aluminum pie pan can become a *tambourine*. With scissors, poke 6 holes around the edge of the pan. Thread buttons on pieces of yarn, and attach the pieces to the pan by threading the yarn through the holes and tying firm knots. Ole! Ole!

A small box without a lid (shoe box or cigar box) can become an *instant guitar*. Place five or six rubber bands around the box and plunk out a song. Note that bands of different thicknesses make different sounds.

Use a clean comb to make a *mock kazoo*. Cut a strip of waxed paper the length of the comb. Hold the strip tightly across the teeth of the comb and blow a tune against the uncovered side of the teeth.

A cylindrical oatmeal box makes a fine *drum* if you hit it with wood chopsticks.

Any glass soda-pop bottle can be blown across the top for a *whistle*.

Jam and mayonnaise jars of different sizes can be filled with water at different levels and tapped gently on the side with metal spoons—to make bell-like *notes of the scale*. You can add a different drop of food coloring to each jar to help your child distinguish different tones.

I don't ever make a special trip to the grocery store to collect items such as I've just listed. And I don't think you have to, either, if when you are shopping, you just keep an eye out for containers that can be recycled into playthings rather than junked into the garbage can. "Double-duty marketing" can provide you with an ample supply of materials for making things at home, saving time and money.

To inspire my family's imagination (and to teach conservation), I keep a large packing box in the kitchen labelled "Recycle Me" right next to the garbage can. Any time anyone empties a box or bottle that could be reused for making a toy, it goes into the box instead of into the garbage. What follows in this chapter are some of *Romper Room*'s most successful "recipes" for homemade toys.

MAGNIFICENT MILK CARTONS

A humble half-gallon cardboard milk carton can be infinitely resurrected. Here are five reincarnations. The first uses a paper-towel tube as well.

Little Farm on the Prairie

To construct two farm buildings and a silo, you will need:

    red construction paper
    1 paper-towel tube
    1 ½-gallon milk carton
    glue or paste
    scissors
    Magic Markers or crayons

Cut off the bottom third of the milk carton. Now you have 2 buildings that can become a barn and a shed.

Cover both pieces of the carton with red construction paper (glue on). Then use a Magic Marker or a crayon to decorate the buildings with doors, windows, and lines that look like barn siding.

The paper-towel tube is going to be the silo. Cover the tube with red construction paper, gluing it on carefully as you did on the barn. Leave about a ¼" uncovered at the top.

Slit the uncovered portion of the tube in 6 places, and bend the resulting flaps outward.

Make a cone from the red construction paper to fit on top of the silo tube and glue it in place (this is the roof). Draw lines around the tube, as shown below, and draw a ladder leading to a door at the top.

Now the young farmer can arrange the buildings in any way he wants. He can also add a weather vane and lightning rods (made of toothpicks).

Milk-carton Church

If you and your child enjoyed making the farm buildings, you might want to try a church.

MATERIALS:
    1 ½-gallon milk carton
    scissors
    glue
    construction paper (any color); or any leftover wrapping paper (even a grocery bag will do)
    crayons

Cut off the bottom third of the carton. Cover both pieces with paper. Attach the two buildings by gluing them together, side by side. Decorate the buildings by drawing on windows, bricks, etc.

Shed

Barn

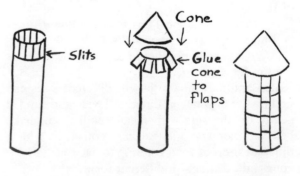

Silo

Cut out the shape of a door. If you want to be more elaborate, help your child color the windows in different colors so that they look like stained glass.

Milk-carton Bowling

Bowling without noisy pins and balls? Yes, indoors in your own kitchen or hall "alley," with easily made tenpins from half-gallon milk cartons knocked over with soft Nerf balls. This is a wonderful indoor game for one, two, or as-many-as-you-can-handle children. Grown-ups will enjoy it, too.

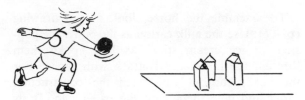

The simplest way to play is to stand up an empty clean milk carton at the end of a scatter rug; then show your child how to roll a Nerf ball or a rolled-up "sock" ball toward it to knock it over. Scoring is simple: hit or miss!

For a classy set of homemade tenpins, try the following directions.

MATERIALS:
10 ½-gallon milk cartons (obviously, the straight kind without handles, not plastic ones)
construction paper: sheets of different colors
cutout pictures from magazines, stickers, decals, etc.
glue stick
scissors
crayons and Magic Markers
AND TO PLAY THE GAME:
Nerf balls or sock balls
a small area rug

To make the bowling pins, cover the cartons with different colors of construction paper, using the glue stick to attach the paper securely. Give each child a pin to decorate with cutouts or stickers that will stay on when a ball is thrown at the carton. Crayons and Magic Markers can be used to embellish the decorations; draw on numbers if you wish.

Now set up the "pins" in your indoor alley. A hall is an ideal spot. To mark the lane, try using a small area rug (small children can't roll the ball too far with much accuracy).

The object of the game is for each child to knock down as many of the pins as he can when he has his turn with the ball. You can help the children keep score, if they like (this can be fun at a birthday party, for example), or just let them have fun taking turns rolling the ball.

This is a good rainy-day game, too, and you might want to save the cartons for just that occasion. After the children have finished playing, store the cartons in a grocery box or shopping bag until the next time they have to stay indoors because of bad weather.

Milk-carton Horse

Your young cowboy can easily construct a corral full of mustangs with just a little bit of help from you.

MATERIALS:
1 quart-sized milk carton
1 small paper cup (or yogurt cup or ice cream cup)
popsicle or ice cream sticks
masking or Scotch tape
Magic Marker
yarn (for tail)
construction paper (for ears)
glue stick
scissors

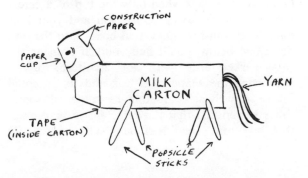

To assemble the horse, look at the drawing (p. 47). Use the milk carton as the body, the popsicle or ice cream sticks as legs (poke them through the bottom and attach with tape). For the head, cut out ears from the construction paper and glue them onto the paper cup. Draw eyes, nose, and mouth to make a face on the cup. Then attach the cup with tape to the pointed end of the milk carton. For a tail, attach 3″ lengths of yarn with a glue stick to the bottom of the carton. Now there's a noble nag!

Children who are horse-crazy can make several of these—to play cowboys and Indians, to populate a farmyard, even to stage a kitchen Derby Day race. But most important, making the horse may also trigger a child's imagination into seeing what other animals he can invent by combining the simple adaptable milk carton "body" box with other discards that usually end up in a wastebasket.

For example:

TRY AN ELEPHANT:
(add a paper trunk and large ears to the paper-cup head—a twisted paper straw for a tail)

OR A GIRAFFE:
(cut the carton in half and fold in the bottom, for a short body and to make the legs

look longer; use a toilet-paper tube for a neck; cut down a paper cup for a smaller head; add small paper ears and a braided yarn tail)

FOR A PORCUPINE:
(punch holes in the carton and insert drinking straws cut in half)

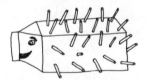

AND FOR AN ALLIGATOR:
(place the carton on its side and cut a scary jaw that opens and closes; draw beady eyes on carton with Magic Marker)

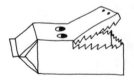

SENSATIONAL CEREAL BOXES

Gone are the days when only the top of a cereal box was worth saving. Once you and your kids have tried transforming cereal boxes into the toys described below, you'll find yourself cruising the supermarket aisle with an architect's eye—appraising the shape of a box and its potential future as well as evaluating its contents! Sometimes I even find that I'm reluctant to mail away that box top! The ideas here start with easily

made blocks, progress to buildings for a play village, then graduate to a doll cradle.

Cereal-box Blocks

Preschoolers love building bridges and towers out of large lightweight cardboard blocks, available in toy stores, but very costly. Try making some of your own with leftover cereal boxes. If

your children like these blocks, you can make even bigger ones out of any cardboard box: gift boxes or grocery boxes, for example.

MATERIALS:
  a rectangular cereal box
  brightly colored construction paper
  crayons or Magic Markers
  scissors
  glue stick

To dress up the box and hide the labels, help your child cut construction paper to cover the box. Here's how to make the cover-up pieces of paper:

First, paper clip 2 pieces of construction paper together (so that you have a double-thickness; this procedure is just to simplify the cutting).

Next, stand the cereal box upright on the top piece of paper near one edge. Use the crayon or Magic Marker to trace around the 4 sides of the bottom of the box.

Now place the cereal box on its side on an unmarked portion of the paper—and again use the crayon to trace around the four edges.

Finally, lay the cereal box on its flat side (front or back panel) on the remainder of the paper, and trace those 4 edges with the crayon.

Now you should have 3 rectangular outlines drawn on the paper.

Use the scissors to cut out the figures, and you will have 6 pieces of paper, one to cover each

side of the box. Help your child match the pieces of paper to the appropriate sides of the box, gluing on one at a time. Now you have a cereal-box block.

In order to build bridges and towers, you will want to make several of these blocks. If your child likes to draw, he can decorate them with crayon pictures or numbers. I've found that using a different color paper for each block also helps to teach children to recognize colors.

Old-fashioned Little Red Schoolhouse

Small children are always intrigued by where other children go to school. Although many American children attend classes in large sophisticated buildings, you might find it fun to tell your kids about old-time small country schoolhouses, many of which are still in use today. To illustrate, here are directions for making one of your own.

MATERIALS:
  1 cereal box
  scissors
  Scotch tape
  red construction paper
  glue stick
  black crayon or Magic Marker

Cut off the 4 flaps (pieces of cardboard that form the box top). Then use the crayon to draw lines on the front and the back of the box so that you can cut the shape of the roof.

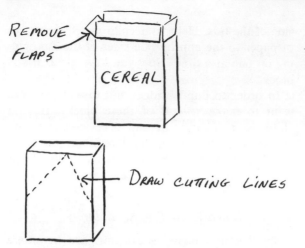

Cut the front panel of the cereal box, being sure to leave the sides intact (you will need these to close in the roof). Cut the back panel of the box in just the same way.

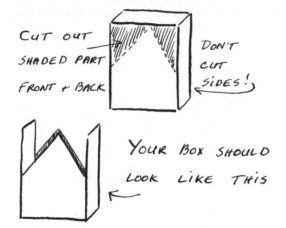

Now bend the side flaps (A and B) to meet at the peak of the roof (C). Scotch tape the sides together. Scotch tape the front and back panels to the folded side flaps so that the roof is closed in.

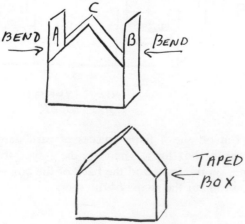

Now you have something that looks like a building! Cover the box by pasting red construction paper on each of the four sides and on the roof. You can make this project easier for your child if you cut the pieces to fit the panels and then let him paste them on (next time he will then know how to do it for himself).

To complete the school, use crayons to draw windows, doors, flower boxes, etc. If you make the windows large enough, you or your child can draw on one of them a face looking out! For a touch of whimsy, draw a tiny American flag. Scotch tape it to a toothpick or a straw for a flagpole, and tape the flagpole to the roof of the schoolhouse. And don't forget you can make a door that opens by cutting a flap along lines you have drawn.

Play Street and Village

If your child has already made the milk-carton farm and church (described earlier in this chapter), by the time he completes the cereal-box schoolhouse he will have three buildings for the beginnings of a play village. Let him use his creativity to dream up other buildings made from milk cartons, cereal boxes, even old shoe boxes. What about a firehouse, a hospital, a movie theater, or a gas station? Three large milk cartons glued together can make a dandy row of apartments. The only limits are his imagination and energy.

Because these buildings are made from lightweight boxes, they can be stored easily between playtimes. Just toss them in one of those indispensable large cartons you picked up the last time you were at the supermarket. On the other hand, your budding city planner may want to display them on a bookshelf in his room.

Oatmeal-box Windmill

Don't forget the cylindrical-shaped cereal boxes in your kitchen. For an energy-saving power plant in your play village, redesign that empty oatmeal box into a windmill.

MATERIALS:
   1 oatmeal box with top
   construction paper or lightweight cardboard
   glue stick

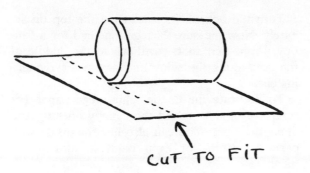

CUT TO FIT

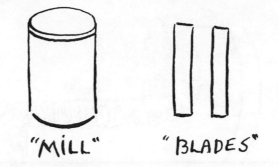

"MILL"　　"BLADES"

scissors
1 round-headed paper fastener
crayons and Magic Markers

Lay the oatmeal box on its side on a piece of construction paper with the bottom lined up with one edge of the paper. Cut away the excess so that the paper will fit the height of the box. Then glue the paper onto the box to cover the labels.

Next, from the construction paper or lightweight cardboard, cut 2 windmill blades, approximately the length of the box and about 2 inches wide.

Now use the scissors to poke a hole in the center of the box. Reach inside the box and insert the paper fastener so that the prongs are sticking outside. Attach the "blades" to the prongs on the outside—and spin! To decorate the windmill, draw on a door and windows. Add tulips around the bottom for a Dutch touch.

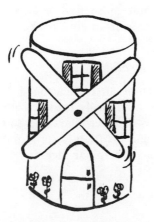

Lighthouse, Airport Tower, Spaceship

Instead of making a windmill, you may want to adapt your covered oatmeal box to another cylindrically shaped building. You don't need blades for a lighthouse or airport tower. Just draw windows around the top. This is a good project to add to the village after a trip to the airport or to a lighthouse. If you don't have either nearby, try to find a picture in a magazine to show your child.

For children who are intrigued by space travel, make the box into a simple rocket booster. Attach a paper nose cone to the top of the box and paper fins to the bottom.

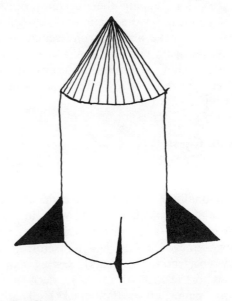

Doll Cradle

A large oatmeal box is just the right size and shape for an old-fashioned doll cradle. Because the cutting requires an X-acto knife or razor, this is a project for an adult to make, and for a child to watch and play with later.

MATERIALS:
  1 large oatmeal box
  glue stick
  X-acto knife or single-edge razor blade
  crepe paper or scraps of cloth from your
     sewing basket
  ribbon for a bow

Turn the box on its side. Glue the top on securely. Now measure 2″ from one end for a canopy. From that spot, cut down to the middle of the box, along the sides, and across the remaining end.

To decorate the cradle, glue crepe paper (or scraps of cloth) around the canopy opening and along the sides. You can also line the inside with paper or cloth—or even paint it with poster paint.

ELEGANT EGG CARTONS

Perhaps you have already discovered that an empty egg carton makes a nifty organizer . . . for buttons, kitchen nails, etc. Children love them, too, for keeping their secret possessions safe. If you cut up the sections of an egg box, you can also make all kinds of fascinating creatures. Never again will you look at an egg carton without imagining a dozen little heads staring at you! Here are three of my favorite ideas of what to do with egg cartons.

Treasure Chest

Those little pockets that hold eggs are just right for storing a child's tiny treasures in his own personalized chest. If your child enjoys the results of this project, he might want to make a similar chest for a friend for a birthday present. A grown-up would also find it useful: to hold jewelry (perfect for earrings), sewing materials (buttons or spools of thread), desk supplies (stamps, paper clips, thumbtacks). This is a good activity for a rainy day when you have lots of time and patience, but the finished "treasure chest" is well worth the extra effort.

MATERIALS:
   1 egg carton
   wrapping paper, construction paper, or fabric
   scissors
   glue stick
   Magic Marker
   paint and paint brush (watercolors or poster paint)

Cut out pieces of paper or fabric to fit the top and sides of the lid of the egg carton. Coat the sides and top of the lid with glue. Then carefully place the paper or fabric covering over the entire lid, pressing it down firmly. Fold over the end pieces as you would the corners on a package, also pressing them down securely.

Next, open the lid and cut out fabric where it covers the holes that enable the lid to snap closed.

Paint the inside of the cups a bright color—or, if you are especially ambitious, line them with fabric to match the top of the box. Finally, write the child's name on the lid of the box with a Magic Marker that will show on top of the fabric. Now you have a splendid chest to keep a collection of coins or shells—or a safe place to empty the treasures from your pocket.

Egg-carton Caterpillar

The segments of an egg carton are ideal for transforming into an easily made creature with a segmented body—a caterpillar. These are so simple your child and his friends may want to make several to stage a caterpillar race.

MATERIALS:
   1 egg carton
   scissors
   paint or Magic Markers
   pencil
   pipe cleaners

Remove the lid from the egg carton. Cut the bottom in half lengthwise so that you have 2 strips of 6 egg cups each—the makings of 2 caterpillars.

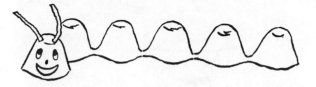

Turn one strip upside down so that the "bumps" stick up. Use the Magic Marker or paint to draw a face on the first "bump." Paint the rest of the cups a different color. Use the pencil to poke 2 holes above the eyes. Thread a pipe cleaner in one hole and out the other so that the caterpillar has antennae.

Since you have 2 strips to work with, this is a good project for you to do alongside each other. If you demonstrate each step, it will be easy for your child to follow your example so that you each end up with a caterpillar at about the same time.

Tulip Bouquet

For a dozen tulips that will bloom all year round, help your child to make artificial flowers from single egg-carton cups. This little bouquet is not only an attractive decoration for somewhere in the house—in a child's room or on the kitchen table, for example—but is also an easily made

gift guaranteed to be admired by grandmothers and other grown-ups.

MATERIALS:
    1 egg carton
    scissors
    pencil
    watercolors or poster paint
    pipe cleaners
    green construction paper
    glue, paste, or Scotch tape

Cut up the egg carton into single segments, discarding the top of the box. Use the pencil to poke a hole in the bottom of each cup. For colorful blossoms, help your child to paint each egg cup a different bright color. Then, for stems, slide a pipe cleaner into the hole in each cup and knot it on the inside to anchor it. For leaves, cut out leaf shapes from the green construction paper and attach them to the stems with glue, paste, or Scotch tape.

If you wish to present a hand-carried bouquet, use another pipe cleaner to tie the stems together, and tie a ribbon bow around the stems. Otherwise, find a small vase or coffee mug to hold the tulips (or make a container from a milk carton or tin can). Either way, say it with flowers!

TERRIFIC PAPER-TOWEL TUBES

Almost anything you throw away, as I'm sure you've discovered by now, can be recycled into some kind of animal. The paper-towel tube is no exception. More obvious uses for the tube are a homemade telescope and movie reels, directions for which follow.

Towel-tube Animals

What kind of animal has a long thin neck that looks like a paper-towel tube? A giraffe, of course. To make an instant kitchen giraffe, simply put a paper cup on top of a towel tube. Draw a face on the cup. Use brown and yellow Magic Markers to color the camouflage spots on the giraffe's body. And use your imagination to make him come alive!

If you answered "people," you weren't too far off-base. The towel tube can be used as the "body" of almost anything. To make boys, girls,

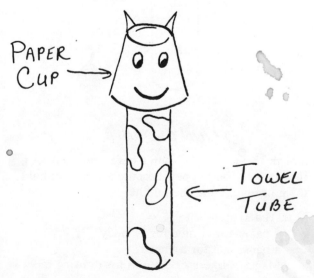

witches, Santa Clauses, or spacemen, simply add a paper cup to a tube for a head. Glue on yarn hair, cotton beards, paper skirts or capes. Al-

YARN HAIR

NEWSPAPER COMIC STRIP SKIRT (PLEATED LIKE FAN)

"FUNNY PAPER" LADY

BLACK CONSTRUCTION PAPER HAT

PAPER OR CLOTH CAPE

COLOR TUBE BLACK

"WICKED WITCH"

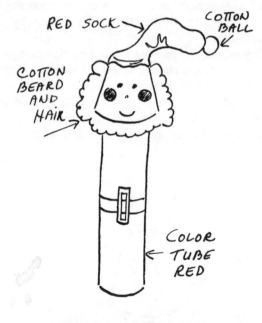

RED SOCK

COTTON BALL

COTTON BEARD AND HAIR

COLOR TUBE RED

"SKINNY SANTA"

though these "people" don't have arms and legs, they make good puppets because a child can hold them firmly around the middle.

MATERIALS:
a paper-towel tube for a "body"
a paper cup for a "head"
Magic Markers or crayons for drawing faces
yarn for hair
paper or fabric for "clothes" or "ears"
glue to attach the above

Telescope

The next time your child asks, "What's on the moon?" you might explain about how scientists look at the moon and stars with telescopes—special lenses that greatly enlarge objects in outer space, so far away that your eyes can't see them at all. Questions about what's out there in space are a perfect opportunity for a trip to a planetarium, if there is one near where you live.

To amuse your budding Galileo at home, show him how to construct his own make-believe telescope out of a paper-towel tube.

MATERIALS:
a paper-towel tube
construction paper
Scotch tape
small piece of plastic wrap
Magic Markers or crayons

Use Magic Markers or crayons to draw designs on the paper-towel tube and on one side of a piece of construction paper. Then roll up the construction paper so that the designs are on the outside. Insert the construction paper roll inside the towel tube and allow the paper to unroll enough so that it touches the inside edge of the towel tube and slides back and forth, like a real telescope. When the paper fits, tape it closed. Fi-

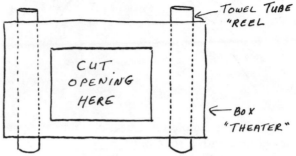

nally, cover the end of the towel tube with a small piece of plastic wrap. Tape the wrap to the tube to represent a telescope lens. When your child looks through the completed "telescope," ask him to imagine what he thinks he can see in "outer space."

Home Movies

As a strategic move in the constant battle against too much television, why not suggest to your kids that they make their own movies to show the rest of the family? This is a good group project—for several children to do together or for a family to all join in. It does, however, require a grown-up to supervise and coordinate.

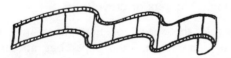

MATERIALS:

a sturdy box (a grocery box the size of a small TV set works well)
2 paper-towel tubes
15′ of plain wrapping paper—or sheets of construction paper taped together—sized to fit the paper-towel tubes
Scotch tape
Magic Markers or crayons

Before attempting to portray a story with a plot sequence of events, you might try out the idea of a "slide" show with a common theme. If the family has recently taken a trip, for example, give each person a sheet of the construction paper (or a cut piece of the wrapping paper) and ask them to draw a picture about the trip. What was funny? Scary? Boring? Can they remember a scene or event? To create suspense, don't let the artists look at each other's drawings until you have taped them together.

Before the drawing begins, you can prepare your "home box office" by cutting holes in the bottom of the cardboard box so that the paper-towel tubes will fit through the holes. Next, cut a very large window out of the side of the box so that the "slides" will show through the opening.

When everyone has finished his picture, tape them all together. Then tape the first one to one end of one of the empty paper-towel tubes. Tape the end of the "slides" to the other paper-towel tube. Then roll up the paper so that the end picture is rolled up on the inside (if you wind the paper up on the right "spool," then you can unroll the paper so that the sequence reads from left to right). Finally, position the box on a table or desk so that you can turn the rolls and show the slides.

If the "slide" idea is a hit, you can then easily progress to putting together pictures that tell a story. For a make-believe story, everyone will have to decide on a general topic. For example, suppose you all decide to depict a jungle adventure. There will have to be some agreement on a main character, but after that, each artist can invent his own exciting episode. When you finally unroll the tale, encourage each artist to supply the accompanying "voiceover" narration.

This is a wonderful rainy-day project for older children to make by themselves. A ten-year-old, for example, could construct his own movie—either by drawing or by pasting pictures on the paper—to entertain smaller children or the rest of the family. As a family project, it works well because even preschoolers can do something to help create the drama—if only to draw a small picture or paste on a cutout.

Steamroller

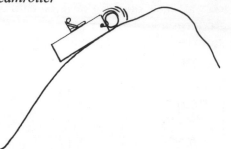

For a very simple toy truck, combine a paper-towel tube with a shoe box.

MATERIALS:
1 paper-towel tube
1 shoe box without lid
construction paper
glue stick
string
scissors

Turn the box upside down so that the bottom of the box will be the top of the truck.

To make the roller, cut the tube so that it is the same width as one end of the box. Pull a length of string through the tube (long enough to leave ends for tying to the box).

To attach the roller, punch a hole in each side of the box near one end. Then thread the loose ends of string through the holes. Pull the string tightly and knot on each end.

Finish off the steamroller by covering the bottom of the box (now the top of the truck) with construction paper. Cut a 2″ square from another color construction paper, and glue it on the covered box for a "driver's seat." Then make a driver by cutting a simple outline figure from construction paper. Fold the driver in half and glue him to the seat. Roll on to action!

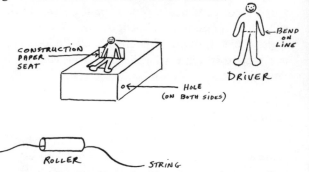

BEAUTIFUL BROWN BAGS

Depending on its size and color, almost any paper shopping bag can be given new life as a stuffed animal or a costume. A preschooler can easily make the paper-bag lion described below. However, you will have to help with the grocery-bag buckskins that follow.

Paper-bag Lion

These directions are for a lion, but the procedure can be used to make all kinds of stuffed animals.

MATERIALS:
1 paper bag (start with a small size; a lunch bag, for example, or a department store paper bag)
old newspapers
2 rubber bands or string
yellow construction paper
kitchen bowl

glue stick
Magic Markers or crayons

Crumple the sheets of newspaper into balls and use them to stuff the paper bag about half full. Put a rubber band or tie a piece of string tightly around the bag to make a neck. Then stuff the rest of the bag with newspapers, and again put on a rubber band or tie a string to close off the bottom.

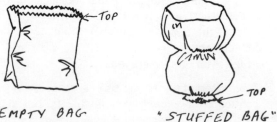

To make a mane for the "lion," place the bowl top side down on the yellow construction paper and draw around it to make a circle. Then on the outside of the circle you have just drawn, draw a wavy line about 2″ around the circle. Now cut out the center along the line of the circle made by the bowl. Next cut along your wavy line. You will have something that looks like a yellow collar.

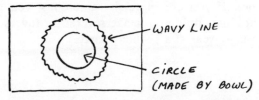

Glue the "mane" on the head of the paper bag. Draw eyes, nose, and a mouth on the face. For a tail, cut a yellow strip from the construction paper and paste it on the back of the bag.

If you begin saving paper bags from your various shopping excursions, you will have a collection that can easily be recycled into a homemade stuffed "zoo."

A pink bag, for instance, makes a perky porky pig. A white bag can be decorated with black stripes to become a zebra or black spots to become a dog (and why not add a black eye patch?). A yellow bag makes a nice cat, especially if you add yarn whiskers above his mouth. Rabbit ears and elephant trunks are easily made from construction paper to create more cuddly creatures.

Paper-bag Buckskins

Fashion fads come and go for grown-ups, but for kids, cowboys and Indians never seem to go out of style. You can show your child how to create his own cowboy suit out of good old brown grocery bags, scissors, and glue.

Here's exactly what you will need:

> 1 large grocery bag for a vest
> 6 smaller ones for chaps (3 for each leg)
> another large grocery bag for fringe for chaps
> scissors
> glue stick and/or Scotch tape

Cut the large grocery bag as illustrated below into a vest with armholes. (Be sure to make the armholes large enough so the child can put the vest on easily without tearing the paper. If you like, you can reinforce the armholes by taping Scotch tape around the opening on both the outside and the inside.) Use the part of the bag that you cut off for making fringe. Glue strips of fringe to both the front and back of the vest.

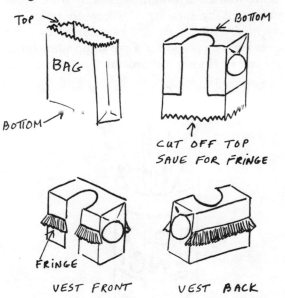

To make the chaps, use 3 of the smaller bags for each leg (or 2 if the child is very short). Cut the bottoms out of the bags, making sure the bags are wide enough for your child's leg to fit inside. Then tape or glue the smaller bags together. Adjust for length by adding an extra bag or cutting off what you have already taped together.

TAPE BAGS TOGETHER

TAPE OR GLUE
TO OUTSIDE OF CHAPS

Use the other large grocery bag to cut a long strip of fringe for each leg. Tape or glue the fringe onto the chaps. Pin the chaps over pants legs, put on the vest, and you have the Lone Ranger!

Paper-bag buckskins are a great project for kids to make together so they can compare costumes. If you are especially ambitious, you and your child could even make several for favors for guests to wear at a birthday party.

CLEVER TIN CANS

The only problem with making toys from metal cans is that they may have sharp edges if the top was not removed carefully. Before you use them for any of the following projects, be sure to check the cans and discard any that look dangerous.

Pencil Holder

Start your child toward organizing his crayons and pencils by showing him how to make this easy holder for his desk. This recycled can also makes a good present for a grown-up when birthdays and Christmas roll around.

MATERIALS:
    small frozen-juice can, or small soup can
    glue
    material for covering the can: construction paper, self-stick paper, wrapping paper, wallpaper, fabric
    trimming for the covered can: ribbon, fringe, braid, rickrack, etc.
    scissors

Cover the can by cutting paper or fabric to fit around it, then gluing the covering on securely. Trim the holder with whatever you can find in your sewing basket. This is such a simple project to do that the kids can let their imagination go wild. Success—and pride in one's work—is guaranteed!

Tin-can Printing

I'll be honest. This is a messy, complicated activity, but it's so creative that I think you and your kids will be pleased with the results. Seeing how their own designs come out on paper may also give kids a clue as to how books and wallpapers are printed. You will have to prepare ahead of time the tin-can "printing press," but your child can take over from there.

MATERIALS:
    tin can (any size)
    piece of rope to be glued to can in swirling design
    pie tins (try paper plates if you are feeling secure) to hold poster paints
    poster paints
    sheets of plain wrapping paper (or newspaper)

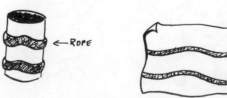

← ROPE

"PRINTED" DESIGN

Glue the piece of rope to the juice can in a swirling design and let it dry. Then show your child how to roll the can in a pan (the pie tin or paper plate) with a little bit of poster paint in it. Now let him pick up the can and roll it along the paper. The rope design will be "printed" on the paper.

OTHER MATERIALS FOR PRINTING:
  a bottle cork
  bottle caps, jar lids
  an empty spool

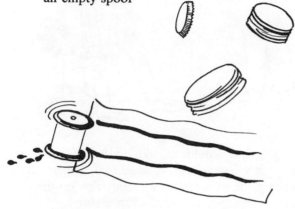

As with the tin can, let your child try dipping the end of a bottle cork into the pan of paint and printing a design. He can also have fun seeing what designs dipped bottle caps, jar lids, and spools make. Spools can roll, caps and lids can make circles. *Both* of you can clean up the mess!

Tin-can Pull Toy

The noise this toy makes may drive you bonkers, but it's gangbusters for preschoolers who can pull it outdoors.

MATERIALS:
  3 1-lb. coffee cans with plastic lids
  heavy tape
  can opener (the kind that punches a hole)
  scissors
  6' piece of clothesline or rope
  small pebbles or stones

Use the can opener to punch a hole (big enough for the clothesline or rope to pass through) in the solid bottom of each coffee can. Next, use the scissors to punch a hole in the center of each plastic lid (again, big enough for the clothesline to pass through). Then, thread one can and its lid on the clothesline.

Next, secure the can at one end by tying a firm knot in the end of the clothesline on the bottom of the can. Stand the can upright and put a handful of pebbles inside to rattle. Now push the lid down firmly and secure it to the can with heavy tape. Tie another knot in the clothesline to secure the first filled can.

Repeat this procedure with the other two cans, spacing them equidistantly on the clothesline. You should, however, leave free at least 2' of clothesline for the child to use as the pull cord. To complete the toy, tie a loop in the free end of the line for a handle. And remember, I warned you about the racket!

INCREDIBLE CONTAINERS

Larger cylindrical paper containers—such as half-gallon ice cream cartons and giant potato chip and pretzel boxes—can inspire kitchen fantasies. Here are a few to make for special occasions.

Tot's Toy Chest

If your family is fond of pretzels and potato chips, you might consider splurging from time to time on the largest-sized round containers you can find in the supermarket. These boxes make dandy toy chests (especially for games that have several small pieces), and are perfect for constructing full-sized head masks for a preschooler (see directions to follow).

To make a toy chest, you will need:

> construction paper
> glue stick
> scissors

Lay the container on the construction paper, and cut it to fit. Then glue the paper on so that all the labels are covered. Let your child decorate as he pleases.

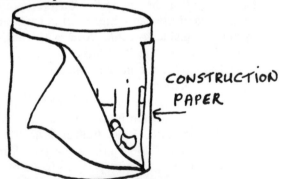

CONSTRUCTION PAPER

These individualized chests can be very useful when children must share a bedroom or playroom. When a child has a personal storage place, he is usually more willing to put his own things away.

Battle Helmets and Animal Masks

If your child likes costumes and disguises, he will love experimenting with these sturdy full-sized head masks. To start his imagination clicking, simply cut holes for eyes in a large potato chip container and put the empty box over his

head. What would he like to be? A growling lion? An astronaut? A medieval knight? Try making one of these for a Hallowe'en get-up—or for any time your child needs a costume.

MATERIALS TO CONSTRUCT A LION MASK:
> 1 large round potato chip or pretzel container
> scissors
> yellow construction paper
> black or brown construction paper
> 1 egg cup from pressed cardboard egg carton
> 6 broom straws
> Scotch tape or glue stick
> black Magic Marker or poster paint

First, cover the box with yellow construction paper and glue it in place. Next, use the scissors to cut diamond-shaped eyeholes.

To make pointed ears, cut ear shapes from the yellow construction paper. Fold the ears in half lengthwise, and tape or glue them, pointing outward, to the top of the box. Then bend the ears up.

For the nose, paint or color black with the Magic Marker the egg cup. Use the egg cup as a guide to draw a half circle on the front of the box where the nose will be placed. Cut the half circle with the scissors. Now use the scissors to punch 3 holes on each side of the egg cup. Insert 2 broom straws (for whiskers) through each

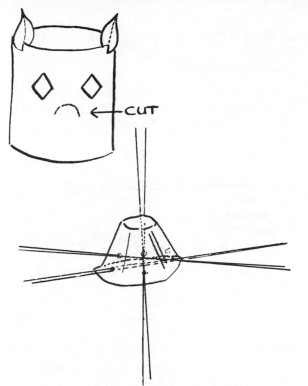

To construct helmets for young spacemen or knights, follow the same procedure of cutting eyeholes. For a knight, cut a straight-across slit, about 2″ high and 6″ wide. For an astronaut, you may wish to cut out a large face-sized opening. For an outer-space goblin, try large round eyes with wavy edges.

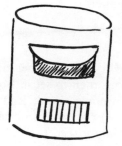

" MIDIEVAL KNIGHT "

hole, making sure they go all the way through the holes on the opposite side of the egg cup. Next, insert the egg cup in the slot cut for the nose. If necessary to hold it securely, tape the cup firmly in place on the inside of the box.

" ASTRONAUT "

For armored helmets or unusual creatures, aluminum foil works best as the covering material. Cut visors for knights or ears for goblins from aluminum pie plates. One of the best ways to enjoy this project is for you to assemble a variety of materials first, then let the kids design their own fantastic faces.

LION MASK

To complete the lionine face, draw a mouth and some freckles beneath the whiskered nose. To create the mane that frames the face, cut two strips of construction paper (black or brown—even a piece of brown grocery bag will do) the length of the carton and about 4″ wide. On each strip cut slashes to look like a fringe. Tape or glue the strips to each side of the mask in front of the ears. Bend out the slashed sections of paper and curl them to complete your cunning lion.

" SPACE GOBLIN "

AMAZING ALUMINUM TINS

Most of us save frozen dinner tins and pie plates if only for toting picnic food or to hold leftovers in the refrigerator. The material from which they are made is ideal for recycling into toys. It is pliable enough to be easily cut or bent into shapes, yet more durable than paper.

Dish Gardens

The compartments of a frozen dinner tin are perfect for a tiny indoor garden to set in front of a kitchen or bedroom window. Don't lead your child to expect that he can cut flowers or harvest vegetables from his miniature seed patch, but he can enjoy seeing shoots sprout up.

MATERIALS:
1 frozen dinner tin
sunflower seeds
soil (small bag of potting soil from a garden store)

Help your child to fill each of the sections of the dinner tin with a small amount of soil. Let him place 2 or 3 sunflower seeds in each section, covering them over with soil. Water—and watch them grow!

Obviously, almost any usually discarded container can be recycled into a dish garden. Try an egg carton, a cottage-cheese carton, a milk carton cut in half. I like sunflower seeds best because they are sure to sprout in a short time.

Potholder Rack

Preschoolers seem to enjoy making these racks for mother and father "chefs." They are also good gifts for the other grown-ups on a child's Christmas list.

MATERIALS:
2 aluminum pie plates (or paper plates) the same size
scissors
stapler
yarn, ribbon, or cord

Use the scissors to cut one of the plates in half. Then place the half plate on top of the whole plate with their insides facing each other. Use the stapler to fasten the half plate to the whole plate. With the scissors, punch a hole in the top rim of the whole plate. Thread a brightly colored piece of yarn or ribbon through the hole and tie in a bow, leaving a loop for hanging the rack.

(If you use paper plates instead of aluminum ones, your child can decorate the rack with drawings or paste-on pictures. Instead of giving the rack away, he may prefer to keep it as a holder for his own crayons.)

Suits of Armor

To go with his knight helmet, your child might want to outfit himself in this suit of mail made from aluminum pie tins or dinner tins. It's a bit complicated for a preschooler, but an older child who can easily tie knots in string might find it fun to try.

MATERIALS:
8 frozen dinner tins for the suit of "mail"
1 frozen dinner tin for a "shield"
scissors
sturdy string or twine
belt (optional)

What you will be making is a kind of "sandwich" board, pieced together with the dinner tins (you can try this with pie tins, too, if you like) connected by lengths of string. To make the front, place four of the tins in front of you down flat. With the scissors, punch a hole in the corner of each tin (4 holes in each). Now cut lengths of twine to connect the tins, as in the diagram below (4" is a good length to start with; you may want to adjust the length depending on the size of the young knight's chest).

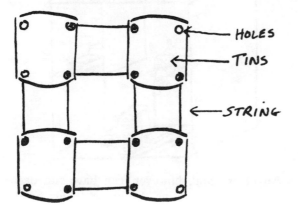

When you have connected the 4 pieces of the front, repeat the same procedure for the back.

To attach the front to the back, cut shoulder straps from the twine and thread them through the top holes of the dinner tins of each side of the "sandwich." Adjust the length of the straps before knotting to make sure the "mail" is covering your child's chest.

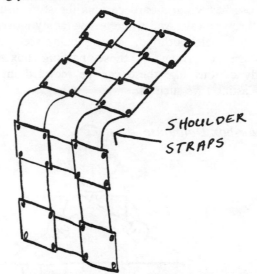

To hold the armor on your child's body securely, you can tie a piece of twine around his waist; even fasten it to the holes in the tins. That's just a little bit too stringy for me, however. I prefer to simply fasten a belt around his waist to keep the mail from flapping.

For a final touch of self-protection, use another dinner tin or pie plate to make a shield. Punch 2 holes on opposite sides of the tin and thread through a piece of twine. Knot tightly so that he will have a secure handle. On to battle!

GORGEOUS GROCERY BOXES

Whenever I go to the supermarket or liquor store, I try to have some of my purchases packed in those heavy cardboard cartons the store usually throws away. And when a new family moves into the neighborhood, you should see me scrounge for some of those packing boxes! Sturdy cartons like these can be recycled into long-lasting toys such as:

Liquor-box Dollhouse

A case-sized liquor box with its cardboard partitions for a dozen bottles can easily be adapted to a six-room, two-floor dollhouse. Here's how:

MATERIALS:
   1 case-sized wine or liquor box with cardboard partitions for 12 bottles
   heavy masking tape
   scissors

Cut the lid off the box. Save it to make a gabled "roof" later. Now stand the box on its end so that the sections for 3 bottles are at the top (or roof) and the sections for 4 bottles are on the side.

Remove 2 of the horizontal pieces of cardboard. This leaves you with the middle horizontal piece in place as the "second" floor of the house; the two vertical pieces are now "walls"

for four large rooms, and two small central rooms.

The next step would obviously be to tape the second floor and walls firmly in place. If your child's dolls like roughing it, the house is ready for them to move in. It's sometimes a good idea to do this anyway so that your child, especially a preschooler, can get the "feel" of the house and decide how he wants to use the rooms. He may, for instance, decide that the box would make a better garage for his trucks (or army barracks for soldiers) than a home for whatever little figures he plays with!

An older child, however, can have fun decorating and redecorating the house to his heart's content, making it as simple or elaborate as he wishes. If this is the case, you may want to assemble some of the following:

   poster paint—for walls
   scraps of fabric, wrapping paper, wallpaper
     —for rugs, wallpaper
   picture magazines—for pasting cutouts on the walls
   rickrack, buttons—for wall borders, doorknobs
   glue or paste—for attaching any or all of the above
   crayons or Magic Markers—for drawing windows, doors, pictures
   scissors—for cutting out doors, windows

If you and your child want to decorate the inside of the house, it's easiest to begin the "wallpapering" before you tape in the floors and walls.

One way to do this is to remove all of the partitions and line the inside of the box with paper. Also glue paper to the partitions, being careful to recut the interlocking slits that hold the partitions together. When you have finished your painting and papering, reinsert the partitions, tape them in place, and host a housewarming!

Apartment Houses

For dollhouses with larger rooms, or for kids with several doll families, try stacking and gluing together with cement grocery boxes of the same size. Three boxes (more would be too wobbly, I think) make a three-story townhouse for one family or a three-flat apartment building for three families.

Mini-auto

Once you start constructing vehicles out of grocery boxes, there's no limit to what a child's imagination can conjure up . . . a boat, a plane, even a car of his own. If the train seems simple and too tame, assemble the following materials and help him to put together a sporty preschooler automobile.

MATERIALS:

1 large grocery box
5 paper plates for wheels and steering wheel
2 paper cups for headlights
2 muffin cups for taillights
pipe cleaners
tape, glue stick
construction paper
scissors

PIPE CLEANERS

PAPER CUPS

PAPER PLATES

Cut off or fold in the 4 flaps of the grocery-box car body. Give it wheels by gluing or taping 4 of the paper plates onto the 4 corners of the outside. Add paper-cup headlights to the front of the car and muffin-cup taillights to the back by gluing their bottoms to the box.

For a steering wheel, use the scissors to punch 2 holes in the middle of the paper plate. Thread a pipe cleaner through the holes. Attach the ends of the pipe cleaner to the front edge of the box. Finally, cut 2 rectangles out of the construction paper for license plates. Help your child to write numbers or his name on them to personalize the tags. Glue the plates on the front and back of the car. When your child climbs inside and sits behind the wheel, you're in business.

Packing-box Clubhouse

For a charming cottage or castle that a child can truly call his own, see if you can pick up a large appliance (dishwasher, TV set, etc.) packing box. Better yet, keep your eyes open for someone in your neighborhood who may be trying to get rid of one. You will have to do most of the work on this building as it requires heavy cutting for doors and windows, but the kids can do all the decorating. Before you begin, however, be sure to remind the children never to get inside a box like this until you have cut the openings. It could accidentally close on them and cut off their air.

MATERIALS:

1 large appliance packing box
X-acto knife or strong scissors for cutting
paint and/or Magic Markers

Start by cutting off only 1 of the 4 box flaps (this is the side you will use for the doorway). Then stand the box on end with its open side down and the remaining 3 flaps extended on the ground (for balance). On the side without a flap, cut a large doorway so that kids can go in and out. Opposite the door, cut a small window so that children can look out when they are inside.

Now your work is finished. Get out the paint pots and Magic Markers and let the kids go to work embellishing the building. For a cottage,

suggest they draw shutters for the window, windowboxes, and flowers and shrubs around the base. For a castle, they can draw boulders and attach pennant flags (if you plan a fort or castle, by the way, you may want to make slit windows instead of a big square one). If the box is destined to be a clubhouse, they may want to glue pictures on the outside. Let them do it their way.

CHAPTER FIVE

Housebound?
Things to Do Indoors

Preview:

THREE EASY PUPPETS

THREE STEPS TO A PLAY

THE PAPER OFFICE: MORE PAPER TRICKS

RAINY-DAY ROUTINES

SICK IN BED

MORE MAGIC

REMEMBER THE DAY WE MADE . . . ?

GRAND FINALE—INDOOR GYMNASIUM

FAMILIES WITH SMALL CHILDREN USUALLY FIND that time outdoors every day is a must—if only for a walk around the block to let off energy and steam. But occasionally it seems that the fates have condemned you to an indoor pressure cooker. It's raining cats and dogs, or one of the kids is in bed with a cold, or you're stuck at home all day waiting for the plumber to unstop the sink. If you're a working parent, sudden news that the baby-sitter can't show may even mean you have to take your preschooler with you to the office.

Having to stay indoors need not spell disaster.

This can be an ideal time to put your imagination to work—and to appeal to a child's instinctive sense of theater. A touch of play acting or melodrama on your part on a rainy day can make even an ordinary routine—such as fixing lunch—a homemade SRO hit.

In this chapter, I've listed several projects that can, of course, be used anytime—but that you might save for one of those impossible days when you feel confined. To get you started, here are directions for three puppets easily made by preschoolers.

THREE EASY PUPPETS

Clothespin Puppets

This kind of puppet is best made from the old-fashioned kind of wood clothespin with a round head (not the hinged kind). Children have made puppets and dolls from these ever since they appeared on the scene in the last century. If your child enjoys making clothespin puppets, look for one the next time you go to a museum featuring Americana and show him a historical prototype!

MATERIALS:
    wood clothespins with round heads
    pipe cleaners (for arms)
    scraps of fabric and paper (for clothes)
    cotton balls and pieces of yarn (for hair and
      beards)
    Magic Markers or paint (to draw faces)
    scissors
    glue

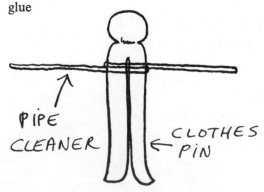

PIPE CLEANER   CLOTHES PIN

Help your child to paint features on the face of the head. Then glue on hair and clothes from scraps of yarn and fabric. Why not make a fam-

ily of these puppets to live in the dollhouse described in Chapter Four? They are just about the right size.

COTTON BEARD AND HAIR

"GRANDFATHER"

Or, make a regiment of look-alike toy soldiers. On the top of each clothespin, glue 1 ball from scraps of ball fringe to look like a furry military hat. Use Magic Markers to draw on chest and pants stripes.

Egg-carton Finger Puppets

Lest you thought we had exhausted the possibilities for egg-carton toys in Chapter Four, here's one more way to recycle an egg box. The cups of a pressed cardboard egg carton are just right for finger-head puppets.

MATERIALS:
1 egg carton
scissors
paint and/or Magic Markers

Help your child to cut the individual cups in the bottom half of an egg carton so that he has a dozen little "heads." He can then use the paint or Magic Markers to draw on faces. Put one head on each finger—and you have quintuplets!

As with the two previously described puppets, if you wish to make these more elaborate, you can glue on cotton or yarn hair, or make paper hats for the egg-cup heads. You can also cut out from construction paper rabbit ears, elephant trunks, etc. to create simple animals.

Glove-finger Puppets

Make use of the odd knitted gloves around your house for a quintet of puppets.

MATERIALS:
1 knitted glove
scissors
scraps of fabric (felt, if you have any) and yarn
small buttons
cement glue
needle and thread

First, cut the fingers off the glove.

Then, sew 2 buttons on each finger for eyes. Sew one button on for a nose.

From the fabric scraps, cut out ears, mouths, tails—even clothes. Make hair, beards, tails from the yarn. Glue or sew the features onto the fingers.

THREE STEPS TO A PLAY

If simple puppets were a hit with your young Bernhardts and Barrymores, you might want to graduate to something more elaborate. The muppet-like sock puppets about to make their debut take more time and help from you, but they are longer lasting. Older children can make them by themselves. And if dramatic action is really your kids' thing, encourage them to construct the grocery-box theater with shirt cardboard scenery that enhances the performance of any puppeteers.

Sock Puppet

I don't know why, but no matter how careful I am, somehow I always end up with unmatched socks in the laundry. These sock puppets make good use of those odd socks—and of outgrown ones, as well.

MATERIALS:
an old sock
cardboard
scissors
crayons or Magic Markers
glue

To make the mouth of your talking puppet, cut a slit in the toe of a sock as shown in the picture on p. 70. Next, cut a piece of cardboard for the mouth in one of the shapes shown.

Fold the cardboard in half, and glue the mouth

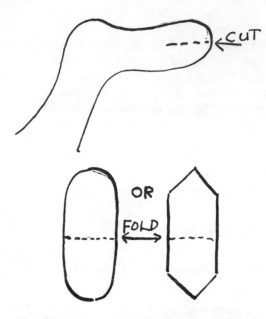

to the slit in the sock. Use the remaining cardboard to cut out eyes (and ears, if you like), and glue them to the sock.

Now show your child how to stick his hand in the sock with his thumb in the bottom part of the mouth and his fingers in the top part. By moving his fingers and thumb, he can make the sock puppet "talk" a blue streak.

To make the puppet look more professional, you can add all kinds of "fancy" embellishments. Use buttons for eyes, for example. Or glue on cotton or yarn hair, beard, whiskers. For a more realistic-looking mouth, color the cardboard red before you glue it into the sock. You can even glue red cloth onto the cardboard mouth and add a glued-on red dragon tongue for a sock monster. The extent to which your child decorates the puppet really depends on his energy and imagination in making use of what odds and ends you have available.

Grocery-box Proscenium Theater

Put your puppets on stage in an empty grocery box. First, cut away the lid. Then simply cut out one side of the box as shown in the picture below so that it looks like a proscenium theater. The actual stage "boards" are whatever surface—a table or the floor—the open side without the lid rests on.

Children can simply move the clothespin or the popsicle puppets about this stage. When they manipulate the sock puppets, however, they would probably prefer to be "invisible," moving the puppets from below the stage surface as do professional puppeteers. You can help them create the illusion by placing the box on two tables behind a sofa. While the children crouch behind the sofa, the audience applauds from the other side.

If you can get your hands on a discarded large washing machine or dryer box (phone one of your local appliance stores), you don't have to worry about a base for the theater. Cut a rectangular hole in the front of the box for the stage opening, cut away the back of the box so that the kids can crouch inside. They can either hold the puppets up for the audience, or move them around on a small table placed inside the box.

Cardboard Scenery

Save pieces of cardboard (cut-away box lids, for example, dress-box tops, or shirt cardboards) to make "flats" for your grocery-box stage. First, cut the pieces of cardboard so that they are about 2″ shorter than the height of the grocery

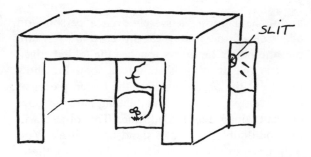

box. Then, cut slits in the "wing" sides of the grocery box—starting the slit at the open bottom and going all the way to within 2″ of the closed top of the box. After your child has drawn whatever scenes he wishes to on the flats—trees for a forest, for example, or furniture—he can insert the flats through the "wing" slits.

THE PAPER OFFICE: MORE PAPER TRICKS

The phone call you have been dreading has finally happened. The baby-sitter, bless her beautiful long-suffering heart, is sick. Despite all of your careful planning for such emergencies, you are due at the office in thirty minutes and it's too late to make other plans for your preschooler (hopefully, there is a friendly neighbor standing by, but I'm imagining the worst). You can't call in sick yourself because you have a meeting scheduled at 10 A.M. that can't be canceled without dire consequences. Face reality. You have to take your child with you to work. Perhaps when you get to the office you can make a phone call that will find a place for him in the afternoon, but until lunchtime when you can sneak away to transport him, you're stuck.

Gather your wits and be positive. It may be inconvenient for you to take your child along to work, but for him, it's a genuine adventure. And in our struggles to be "perfect parents," we often forget that our kids can be much more help than we think. This was never more clearly demonstrated to me than when my two kids—Jenny and Joey—pitched in at work to help me out in a crisis.

One snowy morning a few years ago when we were doing a live *Romper Room* show out of Baltimore, I heard over the radio that both Joey's and Jenny's schools (and Joey was a four-year-old preschooler) were closed for the day. So I had no choice. I bundled them into the car with our dog and took them along with me to the studio. Apparently, the roads throughout the city were icier than I had thought, because not one single child scheduled to appear on the show that day turned up.

As air time approached, there was only one solution. We did the entire show with Joey and Jenny improvising as the *Romper Room* kindergarten, even bringing the dog onto the set as an extra "body" for every segment that involved more than two children. That's one show I hope I never have to repeat, but no doubt about it, the kids were terrific!

You may not work in a television studio, but if you are in any kind of an office, there's bound to be plenty of paper around. Give your child a corner of your desk, and keep him busy and amused with the following simple activities. If in your frenzied departure from home you can remember to bring along a box of crayons and some safety scissors, you've won half the battle.

Folds Quartet

All of these paper tricks can be performed with office stationery and envelopes.

Folded Village

While you make phone calls, let your child fold envelopes to make as many stand-up village buildings as he likes.

MATERIALS:
envelopes
crayons
scissors

Show your preschooler how to fold an envelope in half. Then let him draw a building, a tree, a church, a house, a store—even a person—on one side of the fold with the crayons. Be sure that the object he draws touches the folded edge.

After the drawing is complete, show him how to cut out the object, keeping the folded pieces of the envelope together and making sure he does not cut along the folded line. The object will then be doubled and can stand up by itself. You only have to show him how to do one of these; then he can amuse himself by constructing the rest of the village.

Paper Dolls in a Row

Remember the *first* time you saw someone cut out a row of dolls from a single sheet of paper? It looked like magic. This may be a golden-oldie, but kids love it.

MATERIALS:
   1 sheet of paper (standard 8½″ × 11″ works fine)
   scissors
   crayons

Show your child how to fold a sheet of paper as if you were pleating it for a fan. Check to make sure you have an even number of pleats, and that they are wide enough for drawing (a standard sheet of 8½″ × 11″ office paper will pleat nicely into 6 sections, as in the diagram).

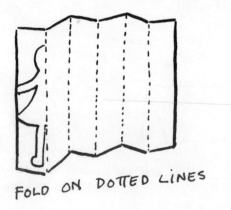

FOLD ON DOTTED LINES

Now with the paper folded up, help your child to draw an outline picture of the half of a doll from head to toe. Be sure that half the face comes on one fold, and the outstretched arm on the unfolded edge of the paper.

Then help him to cut out the doll around her outline, but not on the fold. Unfold the paper, and *voilà*—a row of dolls. Suggest to your child that he use the crayons to draw on faces and color the dolls.

Folded Canoe

For this simple boat—that will float—use a single piece of paper twice as long as it is wide. Cut a standard sheet of 8½″ × 11″ typing paper, for example, into a piece that measures 5″ × 10″.

First, fold the paper in half so that corner "A" touches corner "C" and corner "B" touches corner "D."

Next, fold corner "E" so that it touches line "A–B" and fold corner "F" so that it also touches line "A–B."

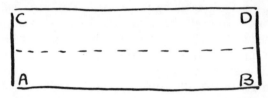

Now fold back the top edge of the paper ("A–B") to dotted line "G"—then fold back once again to dotted line "H."

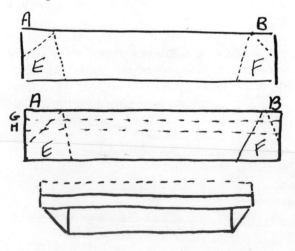

Do the same thing with the other side of the boat.

Now you have a canoe!

To make the bottom of the boat flat—as in a skiff, make one more fold along the bottom edge as in dotted line "J." Fold it toward you first, then away from you, so that it is flexible.

Then, carefully pull apart the gunwales of the skiff—and push in the flat bottom you have made with that last fold. Adjust with your fingers, pinching the corners if necessary until the boat will sit on a flat surface.

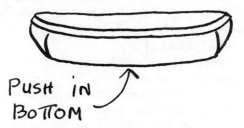

PUSH IN BOTTOM

Your child can take this boat home to add to his bathtub flotilla. Or—be bold and let him christen it in the office bathroom sink! A five-minute try-out probably won't upset anyone.

Several of these flat-bottomed skiffs, by the way, can also be decorated and used for birthday-party favor cups. Try filling them with candy, potato chips, or carrot sticks.

Loop-the-loop Paper Airplane

Here's a paper airplane that will fly in circles. To make it, follow the steps in the picture diagrams below.

MATERIALS:
  a sheet of heavy paper
  scissors
  crayons or Magic Markers
  a paper clip

1. First, fold the paper in half lengthwise.
2. Draw an airplane with wings and a tail, as in picture 2.
3. Draw a line on the plane about 1″ above the fold on each side, as in picture 3.
4. Cut out the airplane shape, being careful not to cut on the line above the fold.

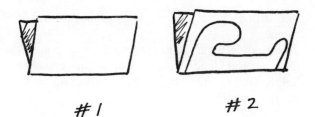

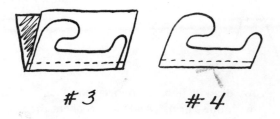

5. Spread out the airplane and color. Show your child how to make airplane markings on each wing tip.
6. Refold the airplane. Now fold down each wing along the line drawn on it, as in picture 6.

To give the plane direction, put a paper clip on its nose. And toss it into the air for a spin!

Your child can make the plane more maneuverable by experimenting with cutting different wing shapes and by putting more than one paper clip on the nose.

Desk Trio

Here are three quiet-time activities that any child can execute sitting behind a desk, even if he is sharing yours!

Star from the Letter A

When children are learning to print letters, they will enjoy transforming the letter shapes into other figures. A capital letter "O," for example, only needs eyes, nose, and mouth to become a friendly face. To make a star—handy in decorating all kinds of paper goodies—show your child how to build on the shape of the capital letter

"A." All you need is a piece of paper and a crayon.

First, show your child how to draw a straight-sided capital letter "A," making the crossbar slightly higher than usual, and extending it so that it looks like "arms."

Now, draw a line to connect one "leg" of the "A" with one "arm." And then connect the other "leg" with the other "arm." *Voilà!* A star!

To keep him busy, suggest to your child that he make a page-full of these simple stars, then color them in different colors. When you go home, you might find a reference book with flags of different countries in it that he can now copy, emblazoning the flags with stars.

Wristwatch

This paper play watch may speed up a pre-schooler's interest in learning how to tell real time. At any rate, it's easy to make and something he can take home from his "hard day at the office."

MATERIALS:
  a piece of paper—heavyweight or con-
    struction paper works best
  crayons and pencil
  scissors
  paper clip

To make the watch face, cut a square of paper about 1½″ × 1½″. With pencil or crayon, draw a square to separate the face from the frame. Next, write the numbers 1 through 12 around the face in a circle. (You might let your child borrow your watch to copy if it is big enough and has a numbered face.)

Since this watch will always tell the same time, ask your child his favorite time of day before drawing in the big and little hands. For example, perhaps his favorite television program comes on at six o'clock in the afternoon. Then draw in the long and short hands to point to the correct numbers. Use the crayons to color the frame around the face for contrast.

To ready the watch for wearing, fold the square paper face in half and cut a small slit on the fold near each end within the watch frame.

Now cut a watch band about 7″ long and ½″ wide from the paper. Insert the band through the slits you have cut on each side of the watch frame. Try the wristwatch on your child's wrist for size, and adjust the fit with a paper clip to fasten the band firmly.

Attaché Case

To take home all the goodies he has made at the office, show your child how to make this easy attaché case of his own.

MATERIALS:
  2 pieces of cardboard approximately 14″ ×
    11″ (the size can be flexible according to
    what you can scrounge up; cardboard
    boxes can be cut up easily as can a ma-
    nila file folder)
  1 piece of paper—heavyweight or con-
    struction paper
  ribbon, pipe cleaners, or string (if that's all
    you can find), for handles
  Scotch tape
  scissors
  crayon

Before you begin, you might show your child your attaché case—if you carry a briefcase to work—and explain to him what you carry in it. The child's version will be a carryall for pictures and papers he wants to save—not just from his day at the office, but also from school or other projects at home.

To make the briefcase, start by taping the 2 pieces of poster board together lengthwise along the bottom edges.

With the scissors, punch 2 corresponding holes near the top center no more than 3″ apart (if you are using pipe cleaner handles, keep the holes small). Push a pipe cleaner or a piece of ribbon through the outside to the inside of the case and knot or twist the ends to secure the handles.

Now cut two triangles out of construction paper and fold as shown below:

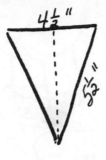

Tape the triangles to the lower half of the case as below:

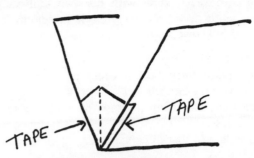

Complete the case with a monogram. Help your child to write his initials (with the crayon) on the attaché case under the handles on both sides.

For further embellishment, the child can add drawings or paste cutout pictures from magazines on the outside of the attaché case. He can use it to store old birthday cards, school papers, pictures of friends, drawings he has made—anything he considers special.

RAINY-DAY ROUTINES

Rainy days bring out the actress in me. If we have to stay indoors because of bad weather, I really encourage the kids to ham up humdrum routines—to soak up the luxury of a long, playful bath—to help prepare an unusual lunch. If bad weather gives you a little extra time with the kids underfoot, take advantage of it!

Bathtub Bonanzas

Soap-suds Sculptures

Children can make their own bars of soap and you can feel artistic by trying our recipe for soap-suds sculpture.

MATERIALS:
  4 cups of Ivory Snow
  ½ cup water
  1 large bowl and hand-operated egg beater
    or large mixing spoon
  newspapers
  towels

Make sure you have plenty of newspapers on hand as this project is guaranteed to be messy.

Begin by placing the Ivory Snow in the mixing bowl. Add a small amount of water and start to mix or beat the soap suds and water. Add only a *tiny* amount of water at a time so that you gradually make a substance that is the consistency of clay or a stiff dough. If you use too much water, you will end up with mush. The object is to have a substance of clay consistency that the kids can mold into shapes such as snowmen, balls, rabbits, bears, etc.

Give each child a few spoonfuls of the "soap clay" on his own sheet of newspaper (double-thickness at least is a good precaution) and let him make it into a shape.

After your child has completed his sculpture, let it sit overnight to dry and become hard. If he doesn't want to use it in the tub as a bar of soap, he can paint it with poster paints and put it on a shelf in his room—or give it to a grandparent for Christmas.

Bath-soap Mitten

You can be sure the kids will be squeaky clean if you equip each child with his own bath-soap mitten, made from old terry-cloth facecloths or pieces of old towels.

MATERIALS:

   1 square terry-cloth facecloth, or piece of old terry-cloth towel

   buttons, ball fringe, scraps of cloth for features

   needle and thread

Fold the facecloth in half. Stitch on the sewing machine or sew by hand around the long open edge and one of the short open edges. Leave the other short edge open so your child can insert his hand.

Turn the washcloth inside out so it looks like a rectangular mitten.

Now, on one side of the cloth make a face by sewing on buttons or ball fringe for eyes and nose. Use scraps of cloth for a mouth and floppy ears.

Insert a small bar of soap into the mitten. Then show your child how to put his hand in the mitten so that the face is on the *back* of his hand while he holds the soap in his palm. Scrub away!

Boats, Boats, Boats

If you have not yet made any of the boats in our bathtub flotilla, a rainy day bathtime is a good chance to try them out. In Chapter One you will find directions for:

   Soap Sailboat

   Nut-shell Boat

   Pea-pod Rowboat

   Matchbox Sailing Regatta

Earlier in this chapter you will find directions for:

   Folded Canoe

If you've gotten the hang of recycling discards into toys, I'm sure that you and your child can invent some nifty boats of your own out of anything that floats. An empty cottage-cheese carton,

for example, can carry toy soldiers or clothespins to dramatize a favorite nursery rhyme: "Rub-a-dub-dub. Three men in a tub!"

Bubble Fun

You don't have to get into the tub to blow these bubbles, but it's a good bathtime game. Let your child take the cup of detergent with him into the tub (use a plastic cup to avoid breakage or make a cup out of an empty milk carton).

MATERIALS:

   ½ cup of liquid detergent

   a large paper clip or a pipe cleaner

To make the "blower," bend half of a large paper clip into an oval or twist a pipe cleaner into a hoop shape with a handle.

Dip the rounded end of the "blower" into the cup of detergent. Blow through the hoop, or wave the hoop through the air to make a stream of bubbles.

Memorable Mini-meals

When you're confined to the house, snacks and meals become times to look forward to, to break up what might seem to be an especially long and trying day.

Whether the weather is bad or not, the "eating between meals" hassle is one I think a lot of parents waste energy fussing about. One way to avoid kids' snitching cookies and snacks while waiting for a late dinner is to stop being rigid about mealtimes—and go ahead and plan an "extra meal" for them. We do this particularly during the summer months when we want to take advantage of the late light evenings to do something outdoors, either by ourselves or with the children. Maybe it would work for you—not just on a rainy day—but more often on a night when you know you won't be home until 8 P.M., but would still like to plan to have dinner with the children.

The trick here is simple psychology—renaming what some people call a "snack" a "meal." The English have made teatime and even "high tea" (a more elaborate tea, sometimes served with sandwiches as well as cakes) a long-honored daily tradition. Why can't busy parents and hungry children in the U.S. do the same?

I try to make the "extra meal" a routine the children expect and can do much of themselves. Every night I check in the refrigerator to see what I have on hand that I can put out for them the next afternoon: cheese and crackers, fruit, peanut butter, cut-up vegetables (celery, carrots, chunks of tomato), occasionally cookies or potato chips, juice, tuna-fish salad made-up and ready to spread.

When we first started planning this extra meal, I also took the time to show them how to slice cheese, to spread tuna fish, to put peanut butter

on celery. It may be obvious, but children do not always know how to do these things instinctively. I also showed them how to clean up after themselves and where to put things away. Our extra mealtime is at 4:30 P.M. Now the children look forward to that time, fix themselves something to eat, and put the makings away, and I'm spared both berating them for snitching and hearing them whine about, "When are we ever going to have dinner?"

On a rainy day, you and your kids might enjoy spending some time in the kitchen experimenting with "extra meals" or with the following simple recipes to jazz up an ordinary lunch. It's a good chance to help your preschooler "chef" graduate from pouring dry cereal out of a box into a bowl to more creative "cooking."

Rainbow Eggs

For a colorful treat, try tinting shelled hard-boiled eggs.

MATERIALS:
  hard-boiled eggs
  food coloring
  white vinegar
  beet juice (drained from a jar of pickled beets)

Boil and shell the eggs. Then color them as you would Easter eggs (only, of course, the shells are off). Do this by putting several drops of food coloring in a cup of water. Add a teaspoon of white vinegar (this makes the eggs absorb the color faster and also fixes the color so it won't rub off). Dip the eggs, one at a time, into the colored water until they are tinted. Blue, green, yellow, and pink are easy to start with. For other colors, consult the back of a box of food coloring.

For especially tasty pink eggs, use beet juice instead of food coloring. Put the beet juice in a bowl, preferably deep enough so that the juice will cover the number of shelled eggs you are planning to tint. Place the eggs in the beet juice, then put the bowl in the refrigerator. While the eggs are chilling, turn them occasionally to make sure they are turning pink all over. When ready to eat, remove the eggs from the juice, drain dry on paper towels, and you have pink eggs.

Rainbow eggs are always fun for kids to make. They are a nice surprise for you to tuck into a lunch box or take on a picnic.

Make Your Own Butter

For a mini-history lesson in how families used to make their own butter, and for a cracker spread we sometimes forget, try this recipe that doesn't even use a churn.

MATERIALS:
  a plastic container with a lid (preferably clear so that you can watch the butter being made)
  ¼ cup unwhipped whipping cream—the heavier the better
  salty crackers

Pour the cream into the container and make sure the lid is on securely. Then take turns with your child (or if you have a group of kids give each one a turn) shaking the container. To get a glob of butter, the container must be shaken for 4 minutes. Stop from time to time to watch what is happening inside the container. At the end of 4 minutes of shaking there will be a ball of butter sitting in the liquid in the container. Pour off the liquid (butterfat), and the butter is ready to eat.

Since the commercial butter children are used to is usually salted, I suggest that you have the kids spread this blander butter on salty crackers for a more familiar taste. (You can, of course, use these ingredients to make your own butter in a blender much more quickly, but kids enjoy doing the shaking and watching the cream actually turn into butter.)

Make Your Own Peanut Butter

Use your electric blender or your Cuisinart, if you are lucky enough to have one, to make this rich-tasting and chunky peanut butter at home.

MATERIALS:
  fresh-roasted peanuts in the shells (enough to yield 1 cup of shelled peanuts)
  1½–3 tablespoons of corn or vegetable oil
  salt to taste

Let the children help you shell the peanuts until you have a full cup. Pour about 1½ tablespoons of the oil into the blender. Slowly add more oil (up to 3 tablespoons for 1 cup of peanuts) if the mixture seems too stiff. Continue grinding until the mixture is as chunky or as smooth as your kids prefer. Add salt to taste.

Make Your Own Raisins

These raisins won't look like the ones that come in boxes—they are larger, lighter in color, and plumper. It also takes four days to make them. But this is a good project for a summer afternoon when you are waiting for the sun to come out the next day.

MATERIALS:
  at least 1 pound of fresh, firm, washed seedless grapes
  a large baking sheet or tray
  a piece of cheesecloth to cover the tray

Help the kids to remove the grapes from the stem, being careful not to squash or bruise them.

Let them arrange the individual grapes in an even single layer on the tray. Then cover the tray of grapes with the cheesecloth, fastening it securely on the sides to keep bugs and dust away.

Place the tray in direct sunlight to dry the grapes—a kitchen window, on a back porch, or an apartment balcony. Make sure that air can circulate freely over and under the tray. You may want to elevate the tray—put it on top of a dish drainer, for example.

After four days, let the kids check the grapes for dryness by pinching them. They should be pliable and leathery. If the grapes are not dry, leave them in the sun and continue to check them each day until they are ready to eat. These raisins, by the way, are better for eating than for cooking.

Peanut-butter Sculpture

If your budding chef wants to combine his culinary skill with his artistic talent, you might experiment with letting him get his hands in this mixture:

MATERIALS:
1 cup peanut butter (your own homemade version or the commercial kind)
⅔ cup honey
1½ cups non-fat powdered milk
paper plates
wet paper towels

Mix together all the ingredients, adding more milk or honey to get a good consistency for modeling. Spoon enough of the mixture onto a paper plate so that the child can create his own sculpture. The wet towels will help to clean off sticky hands before drying them. Children on *Romper Room* have enjoyed making cars, dogs, houses, rabbits, etc.—and then gobbling them up! (You can refrigerate the peanut butter sculptures, but they won't harden and are probably best eaten as soon as they are made.)

Cookies in Shapes

After all of my preaching about how store-bought cookies are just as tasty to the child of a busy parent, you might think the recipe that follows is heresy—but it isn't. A long day indoors is a good chance to act out your fantasy of being

the "perfect parent" . . . to make some simple cookies "from scratch" and help your kids decorate them.

MATERIALS:
for the cookies:
5 tablespoons soft butter
4 tablespoons brown sugar
1 egg
1 teaspoon vanilla
1½ cups flour
¼ teaspoon baking soda

to cut them into shapes:
cookie cutters, or cardboard patterns you and your kids have made

Preheat the oven to 350° F. Mix together until creamy the butter and the brown sugar. In a separate bowl beat the egg and vanilla. Add this mixture to the butter and sugar. Blend thoroughly.

Add 1 cup of the flour and the baking soda to the mixture. Mix in slowly, adding what you need of the remaining flour to make a stiff dough.

Roll out the ball of dough with a floured rolling pin on a floured board or pastry cloth until it is about ¼″ thick. Make sure your hands are floured too, to handle the dough easily.

Now show the kids how to use the cutters or patterns to cut out shapes from the flattened dough. Try some obvious shapes—stars, dogs, boys, and girls—but also use your imagination. You might, for example, trace some of your patterns from a coloring book. Or make a cookie village—of simple houses and trees. This recipe should yield enough dough to make about 2 dozen medium-sized shapes.

Put the cookies on a greased cookie sheet about 1″ apart. Bake for 12–15 minutes, until slightly brown on the edges. Cool, and sprinkle lightly with sugar—plain or tinted with food coloring. Perfect cookies made by a sometime "perfect parent" for "perfect children!"

Gingerbread Men

My favorite old-fashioned cookie is still the traditional gingerbread man. After years of experimenting with everyone's favorite recipe and still not being able to cope with the trickery of molasses, I recommend that you take the shortcut I do—follow the directions for gingerbread cookies on the back of the box of a prepared mix of gingerbread.

The fun of having gingerbread men pop out of the oven is decorating them before and after they are cooked. All you really need, besides the mix, are a gingerbread-man cookie cutter (make your own pattern from cardboard if you don't have one—then cut out shapes with a sharp knife) and raisins for the kids to make faces and suit buttons on the men before they are cooked. For fancier decorating, however, you may want to assemble:

cinnamon candy drops—for mouths and buttons—to be placed on the men before cooking

white and colored icing—to decorate the men after they come out of the oven

chocolate sprinkles, multicolored and silver candy shot, tinted colored sugar, grated coconut, shaved chocolate curls—all to put on top of the icing to make clothes, hair, beards, etc.

For a simple white icing, mix 1 cup of confectioner's sugar with ½ cup solid vegetable shortening. Add more shortening until you have a smooth, spreadable mixture. If it's too gooey, add more sugar—experiment if you have to, to create a workable consistency.

To decorate the men, make an icing tube out of a doubled piece of waxed paper, folded into a cone and Scotch-taped as in the diagram below:

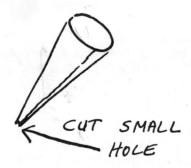

CUT SMALL HOLE

Use scissors to snip a tiny hole at the pointed end of the tube. Then put a few spoonfuls of the icing into the tube. Squeeze the icing down into the hole as with a toothpaste tube. Before attacking the men, practice squirting a few lines of icing on a piece of waxed paper to test the size of the line you will be "drawing." Now proceed to decorate the men with bow ties, collars, cuffs, etc.

To make more elaborate costumes, color globs of the icing with different shades of food coloring. Put a different color in different tubes—and make a blond gingerbread lady with a red dress and green shoes!

This icing is easy and inexpensive, once you get the knack of it. If making it yourself seems overwhelming, take the easy way out. On the baking shelf of your supermarket you will find squirt cans of different colored icing. Even splurging on one can of red can make rosy-cheeked smiling gingerbread people.

SICK IN BED

When a child is really sick, all he probably wants to do is to sleep. But when he's feeling better and getting itchy, here are a few projects to keep him amused. If you provide the materials and a board for him to work on, he'll have no excuse to get out from under the covers.

Jigsaw Puzzles

Whenever I pass by a neighborhood garage sale, I always look for old magazines with colorful pictures in them. These come in handy for countless projects, especially for showing a child how to make his own jigsaw puzzles.

MATERIALS:
old picture magazines
crayons or Magic Markers
lightweight cardboard (the back of a writing pad, for example)
glue stick
scissors
manila envelope (optional)

Let your child spend some time in bed looking through old magazines for interesting pictures. Cut out one of these and glue it to the piece of cardboard. Trim off any excess cardboard so that the backing fits the picture.

Now use a crayon or Magic Marker to draw simple shapes on the magazine picture. Make sure that the shapes are large and that they all connect with intersecting lines. Try to keep the puzzle pieces to no more than six.

Next, let your child cut along the lines so that the puzzle is in pieces. Help him put it back together.

These puzzle pieces are easily stored and kept from being lost in manila mailing envelopes. After the sick day in bed, put them away and save for your next long car trip as a back-seat game.

Alphabet Playing Cards

If your child enjoys playing cards, he might get a kick out of making an alphabet deck of his own.

MATERIALS:
unlined index cards, 4″ × 6″
old magazines
scissors
glue stick
crayons or Magic Markers

First, use the crayons or Magic Markers to write each letter of the alphabet on the individual card. Write it at the top so that ¾ of the card is blank.

Then let your child look through the old magazines to see if he can find a picture of something that begins with each letter. As he finds each picture, he can cut it out and glue it onto the appropriate card. An airplane or apple, for "A," for example. Once you've gotten him started, he can keep busy for quite a while. Suggest that he glue on each picture as he finds it, so that in case he wants to take a break, he will have part of the playing deck completed.

Crazy Notebook

Constructing and flipping through the pages of this book will keep kids busy and chuckling for hours.

MATERIALS:
spiral notebook—copybook size (about 9″ × 6″) or larger
scissors
old magazines
Magic Markers
glue stick

Look through the magazines to find pictures of people or animals about the same size. Cut each picture in half.

Then cut the pages of the notebook in half.

On the first page of the notebook, show your child how to glue the top and the bottom of a picture to the top and bottom of the page. Then, leaving the bottom of the page in place, turn to the second top page and show him how to glue in place the top of another picture so that it matches the bottom of the first. He'll soon catch on to the idea of creating zany combinations of body tops and bottoms.

To make sure the figures match up when he flips the pages of the completed book, I suggest you have him glue all the tops first, then the bottoms. An easier, less accurate way would be simply to paste a picture on each page, then cut the pages in half. Either way, he'll have a wild and crazy notebook to amuse himself and his friends.

Magic Garden

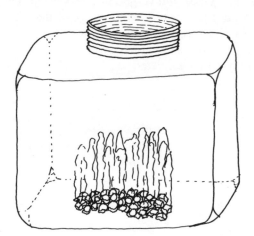

A bed-bound child will be fascinated by this indoor garden, but a grown-up *must* supervise this project because of the potentially dangerous ingredients. (Combining ammonia and Clorox can produce small quantities of toxic fumes, so good ventilation is a necessity.)

MATERIALS:
    a large glass jar or an old fishbowl
    pieces of brick, clay pot, and sponge
    food coloring—red, yellow, blue, green
    4 tablespoons ammonia, 4 tablespoons Clorox, and 4 tablespoons water—mixed
    salt

Moisten the pieces of brick, clay pot, and sponge, and arrange them in the bottom of the container so that they look like a rocky landscape or seascape.

Put a few drops of food coloring on each rock. Use different colors for each rock to create a surreal effect.

Slowly pour the ammonia mixture over the rocks. Finally, sprinkle a generous amount of salt over the landscape.

Put the garden on a bedside table or windowsill where your child can watch it "grow." In five or six hours the rocks will have swollen into unusual colorful shapes. Perhaps the garden will inspire you or your child to make up a story about its imaginary inhabitants.

Muffin-tin Bed Tray

For an instant bed tray, utilize a muffin tin. The 12-cup size works best simply because it is a little bigger and easier to balance on a lap when sitting in bed (for extra steadiness, you can put it on a larger flat tray).

You'll find that a paper cup just fits in one of the muffin molds—a practical way to steady spillable juice or milk. Paper muffin liners are also handy for "disposable dishes" that fit into the molds. The portions they hold may look tiny to you, but remember that small quantities of food can be more appealing to a sick child. Children find this tray amusing because it is different.

MORE MAGIC

A day indoors is a good time for children to increase their repertoire of magic tricks. Perhaps someone will want to put on a show for other kids in the neighborhood on the next rainy day!

Arrow-and-jar Illusion

Say "Presto!" while performing this trick. It looks very mysterious, but takes advantage of a simple principle of physics. The jar of water acts like a camera lens, bending light so that it reverses the image seen by the naked eye.

MATERIALS:
piece of cardboard
black Magic Marker
1 large clear quart-sized jar (such as a mayonnaise jar)
pitcher of water

On the piece of cardboard, draw a very dark arrow about 1″ long.

Stand the cardboard against a book, and put the glass jar in front of it. Your young magician should then ask his audience whether the arrow is pointing right or left. After they answer, he should then fill the jar with water while saying "Presto!"

Now when he asks his audience which way the arrow is pointing, they will discover it is pointing the other way. To repeat the illusion, the magician can empty the jar of water and baffle the audience with another look at the arrow—pointing again in its original direction.

Mystical Rattle Boxes

This is an easy trick that even a four-year-old can perform with poise and aplomb.

MATERIALS:
4 empty paper-clip boxes
a few toothpicks

rubber bands
long-sleeved shirt for the magician

Behind the scenes, place 4 or 5 pieces of toothpicks in one of the paper-clip boxes and put the box inside the magician's shirt sleeve just above his wrist. Fasten the box to his arm with a not-too-tight rubber band. The long sleeve of the shirt will cover the box so that it does not show.

To do the trick, the magician places 3 empty paper-clip boxes on a table in front of him. Then he tells his audience that one of the boxes has toothpicks inside it that rattle and that the other two are empty. To demonstrate, he picks up one box with the arm that has the hidden box on it. When he shakes the empty box, the audience will think it is rattling.

Then, the magician picks up the other two boxes with his other hand and shakes them. They, of course, do not rattle.

Now the magician tells his audience that he will switch the boxes around and that they can then guess which one rattles. No matter which box they choose, the magician can pick it up (with the hand of the arm that does *not* have the hidden box) and it won't rattle. He can have lots of fun mixing up the boxes while the audience continues to guess the right one. Probably the audience won't catch on, but if they do, he can then show them what's up his sleeve and teach them how to do the trick themselves.

Carrot Caper

Next time you're cutting up carrots in the kitchen, use a kitchen towel to give an impromptu demonstration of this simple trick. The magician, of course, will prefer to use a handkerchief when he baffles his audience.

MATERIALS:
handkerchief
small carrot or carrot cut in half to hold in palm of your hand

Cut off a thumb-sized piece of carrot and hold it in your hand. Use your other hand to cover your fist with a handkerchief. Then (also with the other hand) poke the piece of carrot up under the handkerchief so it looks like a "thumb."

Ask your child to take hold of your thumb and pull hard. When he does so, let go of the carrot and pull your hand away, hiding your thumb in your fist. When he looks in the handkerchief he will be very surprised!

REMEMBER THE DAY WE MADE . . . ?

Here are a few special projects to make you forget you *had* to stay indoors. Save them for a time when you want to liven up a housebound day.

Paper-plate Clock

This toy clock is big enough to help you teach a child how to tell time.

MATERIALS:

> paper plate
> construction paper or lightweight cardboard
> round-headed paper fastener
> crayons or Magic Markers
> scissors

Turn a paper plate upside down. On the bottom, show your child how to copy the figures of a clock, putting each number in the correct position.

Cut a large hand and a small hand from construction paper or lightweight cardboard. Use the scissors to punch a hole in the center of the plate. Insert a round-headed paper fastener from the front of the plate to fasten the hands on the bottom of the plate that you are using as a clock face. To decorate the clock, use crayons or Magic Markers to draw a design around the edge of the plate.

Explain to your young clockmaker that the short hand tells us the hour, the long hand tells us the minutes before and after the hour. Keeping the long hand on the number 12, move the short hand around to the other numbers so that the clock tells him it is 8 o'clock, 9 o'clock, etc.

If he can read, you can speed up the time-telling process by writing under the numbers on the paper plate the phrases that we use to say what time it is.

For example, under the one, write, "five after." Under the two write, "ten after," and so on. Under the three write, "quarter past." Under the six write, "half past." Under the seven, write "twenty-five to." Under the nine write, "quarter to."

If the phrases seem confusing at first, don't worry. Eventually, he will catch on—as we all once did. Learning the phrases we use to tell time is like learning a language. Understanding comes as much by rote as it does by logic.

Spool-beads and Belts

If you sew, never throw away empty spools. They can be endlessly recycled into amusing toys. If you don't sew, you can buy several dozen empty spools at a notion shop, often for less than a dollar.

MATERIALS:

> empty spools
> string, yarn, shoelaces
> buttons
> paint or Magic Markers

To make beads and belts, show your child how to thread the spools on lengths of string or yarn. Old shoelaces are handy, too, as the plastic tips assist kids' finger dexterity. Color the beads with paint or Magic Markers and string them with buttons for variety. Spool jewelry makes a handsome birthday gift for a friend.

Railway Engine

This little engine that "can" could pull a shoebox train. It is, however, a charmer in itself.

MATERIALS:

> an empty narrow box with one side open
> 2 pencils
> 3 empty thread spools
> glue
> paint and brush

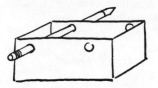

Lay the box on a table with its open side up. With a pencil, make 2 holes at each side near the top at both ends.

Push a pencil through one hole, through a spool, and then through the hole on the other side of the box. Repeat for the other end of the box. Turn the box over, and you have an engine with moving wheels.

To make an old-fashioned smokestack for your locomotive, glue a spool on top at one end of the box. Then paint it a bright color.

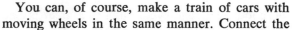

You can, of course, make a train of cars with moving wheels in the same manner. Connect the cars with string or twine as you did the grocery-box train and shoe-box steamroller in Chapter Four.

Bustin' Bronco

Lend your broom to a child for a day to make this western home hobbyhorse.

MATERIALS:
    broom
    small paper bag
    yarn
    glue
    crayons or paint
    scissors
    rubber band or Scotch tape

Paint a horse's face on the bottom of a paper bag, holding the bag so that the horse's face will be right side up when you slide it over the bristles onto the broom handle. Cut small pieces of yarn and paste them to the paper bag head for a mane. Slip the bag over the broom bristles and secure it tightly at the neck with a rubber band or a piece of Scotch tape. Heigh-ho, bronco! for a gallop around the home range.

GRAND FINALE—INDOOR GYMNASIUM

Why is it that when children must stay indoors they have an inexhaustible supply of energy? You can keep them active and happy with a homemade indoor gymnasium—easily set up in the largest room in your house—or better yet, in an empty garage. They may even flock to it on days when they *could* go outside.

You must go to some length to acquire the items on this list, but the extra effort is worth it. Each tool below is guaranteed to channel and dissipate enormous quantities of unused energy.

1. Very Large Packing Boxes

You can obtain these from a moving firm or from an appliance dealer (especially dealers who sell expensive appliances and assemble them for patrons, hence, have leftover boxes). Such a box can become, with the aid of sharp scissors, Magic Markers, and crayons:
    a space ship
    a sailing vessel
    a house
    a cave

an elevator
a camper
a car or bus
a hot-air balloon
an airplane

2. Industrial Cylindrical Packing Containers

Contact your local moving company again, or look through the Yellow Pages for business firms that handle housewares. China and glassware, for example, are sometimes shipped in these "barrels."

To adapt the container to your gym, take the top off the tube and cut off the bottom so that you have what looks like a giant piece of pipe. These tubes are fantastic for rolling over, for crawling through, and for otherwise connecting the rest of your equipment.

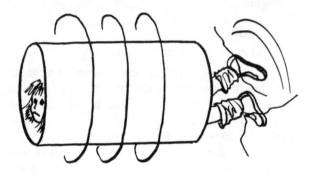

3. Foam-rubber Mats

Order these in large sections—4' × 6' or 5' × 8' from a Sears Roebuck or Montgomery Ward catalogue.

These mats can transform your otherwise empty garage into a mini-Olympics stadium, a mock-trampoline, a wrestling mat, etc.

4. Tractor and Truck Inner Tubes

Again, these are usually easier to order from major catalogues than to scrounge around for. The tubes are terrific for crawling, balancing, and rolling. They make pretend boats in the wintertime, and can be taken in swimming in the summer.

Although you will have to spend some money to equip your indoor gymnasium, you can recoup the cost of the items more quickly than you think —just by avoiding desperation calls to baby-sitters. You will gain happy, relaxed, and tired children, and will become very popular in the neighborhood. A garage gymnasium is a great project for the whole family to assemble together. It is even better when several families chip in to make it a neighborhood venture.

CHAPTER SIX

The Great Outdoors

Preview:
ESSENTIAL PREPARATIONS
BACK-YARD BEGINNINGS
GAMES FOR KIDS AND GROWN-UPS
MINI-SAFARIS
KNOW YOUR NEIGHBORHOOD

YOU DON'T HAVE TO EQUIP YOURSELF FOR AN EX-pedition to Mt. Everest every time you and your child go outdoors, but a few preliminaries can help. A basket by the door for keeping outdoor toys handy—balls, sandpails, toy trucks, etc.—can lessen confusion when it's time to go outside to play as well as help reinforce some sense of order. If you must walk to a park or playground, a wagon, knapsack, or canvas tote bag can keep outdoor gear ready to travel.

In good weather all that most children need to have a good time outside is a place to run and jump and shout. A sandbox, jungle gym, or plastic pool can help, but usually sun and space are enough. When they can let off stored-up energy, things have a way of taking care of themselves. If you have to go to a playground, pack a snack to take along and share—celery or carrot sticks, apples, peanut-butter crackers. If you have a back yard, just open the door—and join the kids when you can.

ESSENTIAL PREPARATIONS

Getting dressed to go outdoors when the weather is nippy can be a lot less of a tangle for both you and your child if you will take a few minutes to show him the following easy routines for putting on a jacket and for putting on boots. These simple skills are guaranteed to boost his confidence —and to send you both on your way "dressed for success!"

Putting On a Jacket

This method will work for any sleeved garment that opens down the front. Demonstrate the steps outlined below and then encourage your child to practice a few times.

1. Place the back of the jacket on the floor. The buttons or zippers are facing up, the jacket collar is in front of the feet, and the sleeves are spread out on each side.

2. Bend over, slip the right hand into the right sleeve, then slip the left hand into the other sleeve. Stand up straight holding the jacket over the head and let it slide down onto the shoulders. The jacket will be on.

It's not important that a child master this technique right away, although most *Romper Room* children catch on fairly quickly. But it is important that the child—and you—know that he can do this all by himself—especially at places like school and other kids' houses where a grown-up may not be readily available to help him get dressed to go outdoors. This is also a real time-saver. (And don't forget, it's a lot easier for a short preschooler to bend over than it is for you!)

And Don't Forget to Wear Your Boots!

Too often a child is likely to walk out of his house and into the rain puddles in his regular shoes because it's just too difficult to put on boots. You can make the process easier and save yourself some worry about colds if you show him how to put on boots with plastic sandwich bags.

The first time, try this method sitting on a chair so the child can be sure to get the left boot

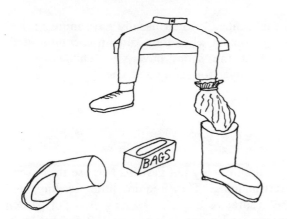

Lift the right boot and slip the right shoe into the toe of the boot. Hold all your fingers on the inside of the back of the boot and pull the boot toward you while pushing the shoe into the boot. Repeat the same procedure with the left boot.

Now help your child to go through the same procedure he has watched you demonstrate.

(Yes, the child does wear the plastic bags inside the boots. When he gets where he is going and wants to take the boots off, you can remind him to stuff the plastic bags inside the empty boots so they will be ready to use when he wants to go outside again.)

Bike Safety—Early Driver Training

" I'M OBSERVING THE 55 MPH LIMIT!"

on the left foot and the right boot on the right foot.

Sit on the chair and place your boots in front of you so that the heels are close to the chair. Explain the obvious—that the shape of the boots is usually the shape of the shoes the child is already wearing. This is so the right boot will fit over the right shoe and the left boot will fit over the left shoe.

Have ready two plastic sandwich bags. Place a sandwich bag over each of your shoes. The bags will make the boots slip on easily without a lot of pushing and tugging. (You might also take this opportunity to remind the child never to put anything plastic near his face.)

When your child learns to ride a tricycle, you can take some time to walk alongside him to emphasize safety rules. Here are the safety rules we have stressed with children on *Romper Room:*

1. Only one child on a bike. Never carry a rider on the back because the bike can tip.

2. Ride only on the sidewalk, never in the street. Check with your local police department for the places a child is permitted to ride. Laws vary!

3. Ride single file—two bikes can bump or take up the whole sidewalk and cause accidents with people trying to walk by.

4. Ride only in the daytime, never at night when bikes must have special equipment and small children are difficult to see.

5. Make sure the bike is the right size—not too large or too small. Accidents happen when a child and a bike are mismatched; a bike of the wrong size is hard to balance and to control.

6. Never play bike games near the street and never show off.

You might follow up a "bike-driver training" session with a visit to a local bicycle shop. Ask the bicycle man to explain how the bike works—pointing out the wheels, pedals, pedal axle, and pedal crank. Children usually have more respect for equipment when they know it is complicated. While at the shop, have your child's tricycle checked over for safety and size.

BACK-YARD BEGINNINGS

If you have a place for a sandbox, a preschooler can amuse himself for hours digging and building. Even on a garden apartment terrace your child could enjoy the sandbox and the pot garden ideas that follow. The compost heap, however, does require some distance from the house.

Tractor-tire Sandbox

You will have to look hard for an old tractor tire, but it makes a great sandbox—complete with edges to sit on. Look in the Yellow Pages for a tractor supply company and see if they can give you a lead. If you live in a rural area, you might be able to find one at a garage that services tractors. When you bring the tire home, you can fill it with play sand—easily available in 50-pound bags at most hardware stores.

Garden in a Pot

If you already have a vegetable or garden flower plot, why not give your preschooler a few square feet of his own to tend? Lettuce, which grows quickly and can be eaten at once, is ideal. A pumpkin patch, if you have the room, is even better. The plant will grow all summer with very little care, flower, and turn into a Hallowe'en pumpkin by September.

If you don't have a garden, or the room for one, try one in a pot. Miniature zinnias and small marigolds will perform nicely, as will lettuce and parsley. Cherry tomatoes are perfect; one plant will provide bountiful fruit that is good to eat.

Children enjoy pot gardens because they aren't overwhelming. They require little weeding, and are decorative as well. As long as a pot garden has sun and water, it is almost 100 percent guaranteed to produce successfully.

Compost Heap

If you have been recycling boxes and bottles into toys, you might like to tell your child about nature's way of reusing our waste. A compost heap is an ecologically sound way of recycling decayed materials to make fertilizer for plants. To make a compost heap, you must save natural leftovers such as: leaves, grass clippings, rinds of oranges, lemons, and limes, fruit cores of apples and pears, coffee grounds, tea leaves (tear open the bag), and egg shells.

Before you start your compost heap, you might assemble some of the ingredients and let your child identify them. He will probably have only one response, "Icky!" or "It stinks!"

Then you can explain that even though we call these things garbage, they are really natural products that can be returned to the soil—to do for plants and trees what good food does for humans. Garbage is not always something to be thrown away!

Take your natural leftovers and place them in a pile in an unused corner of your yard. After a few months, you can spread the material on your garden and around the trees. Selecting things for the compost pile can be one way to make that "it's-your-turn-to-take-out-the-garbage" job more interesting.

Families who live in apartments or who enjoy raising house plants can use coffee grounds and tea leaves on top of the plant soil. It should be applied evenly in a thin layer to help return to the soil natural minerals which the plant absorbs through its roots.

As enthusiastic as I am about making a compost heap, I realize that not all families can be converted. It does smell. It does take time to mature. It does require a corner of a garden. Consequently, when we introduce this concept on *Romper Room,* we always emphasize two points:

1. A compost heap is a *family* project—before you start one, make sure everyone in your whole family agrees.

2. A compost heap is *not* a garbage or a trash heap as we usually think of one. It *is* a pile of natural products returning naturally to the soil.

Peter Pan Shadow Picture

Remember how Peter Pan lost his shadow and went flying into the Darlings' house to look for it? Kids can have fun on a bright sunny day drawing their own shadow pictures.

MATERIALS:
   sheet of wrapping paper about 2′ taller than child—or newspapers taped together for length
   tape (if necessary)

black Magic Marker
scissors

Show your child how to stand with his back to the sun so that his body creates a sharply silhouetted shadow. While he is standing, you can trace his outline on the paper. Then let him cut it out—and take his shadow safely inside so he will still have it on a cloudy day! He can, of course, draw in features and clothes on the shape with crayons if he likes.

How do you equalize the skill, strength, and attention span of little kids and grown-ups? Here are some easy back-yard games and activities in which you can fully participate without being patronizing to your children or losing your dignity.

Shadow Tag

On a sunny day, try this variation of a tag game that even just two people can play. One person is "It." He tries to tag the other person by stepping on his shadow. Then the "tagged shadow" person is it. No fair hiding in the shade. This game guarantees lots of running!

Big and Little Sardines

The whole family can play sardines—indoors or outdoors. It's a good game for a joint family picnic, too, where there might be children of many ages. Let one of the younger ones be "It" to make him feel important.

As I'm sure you remember, "It" goes off by himself to find a hiding place—trying to find a place big enough where everyone playing will be able to squeeze in like "sardines" with him. Everyone else closes his eyes and counts to 100. Then the search begins. The searchers try to sneak into the hiding place with "It," without having the others see them. When the last person has discovered the hiding place, the game is over . . . and can begin again!

Follow-the-leader Musical Parade

You can be the leader the first time—jumping, running, hopping, or whatever at the head of the line of kids and grown-ups. Then let the kids take turns putting the rest of the group through the paces.

For a musical parade, break out the Recycle Rhythm Band (Chapter Four). Now take your place at the head of the line as the drum major, leading the band players with a broomstick for a

WHITE AROUND
EYES AND MOUTH

RED
NOSE

HEAVY BLACK
EYELINES AND
EYEBROWS

RED
MOUTH
OUTLINED IN BLACK

baton. Try to get the kids to follow whatever you
are doing while they are still banging on their instruments.

WHITE MAKEUP
OVER ENTIRE FACE

RED NOSE AND
MOUTH

STARS
AND BUTTERFLIES

Children of All Ages and the Greatest Show on the Block

Why not a back-yard circus? Put a bow on the
dog, let the kids show off somersaults and other
gymnastics, and then you can all make up as
clowns.

Clown Makeup

Save your old makeup—lipstick, cold cream,
eyebrow pencils, eye shadow—for the day you
decide to do this.

You will need to have on hand:

    old makeup as above
    paper cups
    cold cream
    food coloring—red, yellow, green, blue
    teaspoon
    mirror
    powder or flour
    lots of tissues

For each color of makeup, put 2 teaspoons of
cold cream into a paper cup. Add 1 drop of food
coloring and mix with the spoon.

Powder your face and then use the colors to
make round red cheeks, and designs on the

clown face. Add extra touches with lipstick, eye
shadow, and eyebrow pencil.

Clown Faces

Here are some designs you can use.

Best of all, design your own circus clown face.

Home Team T-shirts

Add spirit to back-yard competitive games and
to family get-togethers where games are played
by designing a family logo and printing it on old
T-shirts with raw root vegetables.

MATERIALS:
    raw root vegetables—potatoes work fine
    paring knife
    fabric paint or colored ink pad
    brush
    paper for testing print
    old T-shirts (white undershirts are fine)

A grown-up will probably have to cut the

designs in the potatoes, but all the kids can help with the stamping.

First, slice a clean, washed potato in half. Then use the paring knife to cut away from the surface, leaving a raised design. A star or flower is easy to start with. Or you can try an abstract logo. If the first letter of your team name is a simple one, you can try that, too.

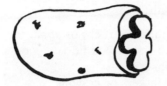

Next, dip the brush in the fabric paint and color the raised design. Or, stamp the potato on the ink pad until the design is covered thoroughly. Let the kids press the stamp down on a piece of paper to test the print.

Finally, stamp the design on the T-shirts in whatever pattern you like. If you plan to use more than one color, I suggest you use a new potato for each color (otherwise, wash and dry thoroughly the original one before trying another color). Let the prints dry well before putting on the T-shirts. After the battle, follow the washing directions that come with the fabric paint.

Butterfly Kite

This simple kite won't fly high or fast enough for competition, but it will delight a preschooler.

MATERIALS:
large sheets of colored construction paper
string
scissors
Magic Markers or crayons

Draw a large butterfly on the paper. Decorate it with Magic Markers and cut it out (for design ideas, find pictures of butterflies in an encyclopedia or nature book).

Poke 2 small holes in the center of the butterfly. Thread the string through the holes and tie. Make sure the string is long enough to let the butterfly really fly on a windy day. Kids will have fun making the kite fly just by running with it in the back yard or on a beach.

MINI-SAFARIS

Little kids can hunt for wild game in their imaginations. But in real life, they can find all kinds of interesting natural things in their back yards, their neighborhoods, wooded parks—or as far afield as you are willing to take them. Here are a few suggestions for preschooler "hunts" and what to do with the "spoils": rocks, leaves, twigs, pods, cones, and berries.

Rock Hunt

Even on the shortest walk, a preschooler can usually pick up at least two or three pretty interesting rocks to begin a collection. Depending on the size of his "quarry," you can show him how to do the following when he gets home.

Pet-rock Zoo

With young children, stick to one rock for simple animals. Monsters, for example, can be made by dabbing paint on odd-shaped rocks. To make a rabbit, let your child glue onto a rock a cotton ball tail and construction paper ears. Then he can add features with paint.

Older children can glue together stones of various sizes to make all kinds of creatures.

FOR A SIMPLE TURTLE, YOU WILL NEED:
6 rocks—1 bigger one for the body, 4 little ones for the feet, 1 medium-sized one for the head
glue
paint or Magic Markers

First, glue the feet onto the turtle. Paint eyes on the head, then glue the head to the body and let it dry.

TO MAKE A FROG, YOU WILL NEED:

5 stones—1 big one for the body, 2 small ones for the legs, 2 tiny pebbles for eyes. Glue them on and paint a straight mouth under the eyes.

Kids can easily make environmental settings for their rock animals. Cut a small pond for the turtle out of a sheet of blue paper or a lily pad for the frog out of green paper. Find a small branch for an owl perch. Let them use their imaginations.

To cage these creatures, and any others they may dream up for a menagerie, show them how to make cages out of small individual-serving size cereal boxes. (Handy, of course, in your kitchen recycle box!)

YOU WILL NEED:

1 cereal box for each cage
Magic Marker
scissors

Use the Magic Marker to draw a cutting line about 1″ away from the edges of the box on both sides. Draw in bars, also. Then cut out along the lines for a cage.

Several of these boxes, of course, can be lined up next to each other to look like a circus train. Making the train may give kids ideas of what kinds of rocks to look for on their next walk to make lions, bears, tigers, etc. If they can't find the right-shaped rock for an elephant, for example, you can fudge a bit. Cut a paper trunk and paper ears from construction paper and glue them on the rock!

Pebble Aquarium

After several rock hunts, your child may have collected a pile of favorites—smooth stones of different colors. To bring out their natural beauty, show him how to wash them and put them in an empty glass jar or bowl. Cover the pebbles with water, add a dash of ammonia, and set the jar in a window with sunlight. The ammoniated water will bring out their natural hues and be an attractive window decoration.

Geologist

The serious young rock-hunter may want to display and label his trophies. He can do this effectively with:

several different rocks of about the same size
a box lid—shoe-box lid is a good size
glue
Magic Markers or crayons

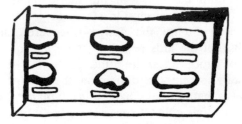

The shoe-box lid acts as a shadow box. Show your child how to lay it flat and to arrange the rocks he prizes most inside the "frame." Leave plenty of space between each rock so they can be seen clearly. If you can't identify the rocks from a reference book, individualize them by writing "names" under them or by labeling each with the date of discovery. Or, let your child draw border outlines around the rocks with crayons or Magic Markers. Then the box of rocks is ready to be shown off.

Rock Bookends

You might want to delegate this project to a baby-sitter when you are away. It is easy and makes a nice present for a brother or sister or grown-up.

MATERIALS:

2 large rocks (about 3″ × 3″) which will sit up
Magic Markers
paint
paint brushes

If you have bookends in the house, show them to your child before you go for the walk to explain how they hold books up. If you don't have any, improvise with anything sturdy (a pair of shoes, for example) just to get the idea across.

On the rock hunt, look for rocks that are not only large and steady, but also fairly smooth. Bring the rocks home and let your child decorate them with Magic Markers and poster paint. A child who enjoys making these for a gift will probably want to make bookends for his own books, too.

Leaf Collecting

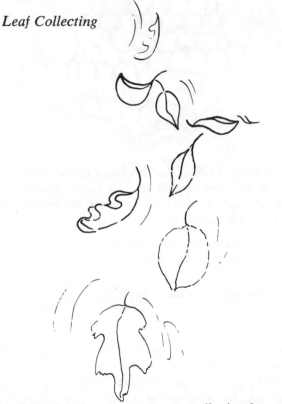

Collecting leaves comes naturally in the autumn when so many different colored leaves are falling to the ground. Here are some ways to save the leaves to cheer you up during a long cold winter.

Pressing Leaves

Leaves that you plan to mount are easier to work with if you collect them when they are slightly damp—perhaps after a rain—and then press them for about a week. To do this, you will need:

    several brightly colored damp leaves
    a pile of thick, heavy books
    for mounting: shoe-box lid and glue and
      Magic Markers

Show your child how to put a damp leaf between the pages of a book. You can protect the pages by inserting a piece of waxed paper on either side of the leaf. For best results—and least damage to books—use only one or two leaves per book. On top of the book with the leaves in it, put at least two other heavy books—and let the book "press" sit for about a week. By then the leaves should be dry and flat.

To mount the leaves, use the inside of a box lid—as with the rocks—and label each leaf by identifying the name of the tree from which it came.

Painting Leaves: Indoor Tree

Your child can make his own tree indoors by painting some of the dried leaves and tying them onto a branch.

    YOU WILL NEED:
      dried leaves
      nicely shaped bare branch
      poster paint and brushes
      milk carton
      clay (ready-made or salt-dough, see Chapter
        One)
      yarn or string
      scissors

To make a base for the tree, cut a milk carton (quart or half-gallon size) in half. In the bottom half, put a wad of clay to hold the "tree" firmly. Insert the branch. If you are making your own salt-dough clay, you will have to wait overnight until the clay has hardened.

If your child wants a tree with multicolored leaves, he can paint the dried leaves with poster

paints and let them dry again. Or, he can use the dried leaves in their natural colors. When the leaves are ready, use the scissors to poke a tiny hole near the leaf stem. Insert a short length of yarn in each leaf and show him how to tie them onto the tree's branches.

Leaf Lady

A novel way to mount special leaves is to make a "leaf lady" on a piece of paper. She can be made from summer or spring green leaves, too.

MATERIALS:
   3 leaves—fairly large one for her dress, smaller one for her hat, one more to cut up for shoes and gloves
   stems for arms and legs
   2 sheets construction paper
   scissors
   glue
   crayons

Maple leaves make the best leaf lady, but tulip-tree leaves, oak, aspen, or any wide leaves will do.

Lay the largest leaf on a sheet of construction paper with the stem at the top. This is the dress. Trim the stem, leaving ¼″ for the lady's neck.

From the other sheet of paper, cut out a circle and use crayons to draw a face on it. Paste the face on the second leaf. Trim the leaf so that it looks like a hat. Lay the face and hat on the sheet of paper with the dress.

Cut stems for legs and arms and lay them in place on the paper. Cut little points from the third leaf. These will be the shoes and gloves.

Lay them in place. Now use the glue to mount the different parts of the leaf lady onto the paper.

Twigs, Pods, and Cones

Whatever object that catches a child's attention on a walk—a smooth twig, a piece of bark, an empty pod, a pine cone—can be brought home to make a nature collage.

FOR THIS YOU WILL NEED:
   a box lid
   glue
   bounty from the mini-safari

Just arranging the pieces and gluing them to the inside of the box lid in a free-form design may please your young collector (as it did with junk sculpture and pieces of wood in Chapter One). But if he is more ambitious, suggest that he use his findings to make a nature scene. Twigs, of course, make miniature trees—and their pieces can make people, animals, and so on. A pod looks like a canoe. A cone can be a tree (you may have to cut a cone in half so it has a flat side for gluing). This kind of "touch-it" project is good for introducing kids to all of the different textures in nature.

Pine-cone Potential

1. Pine cones are just the right shape for shrubs and trees in cereal box villages. Use just as they are—or painted green.

2. Pine cones are natural bird-feeders. Put dabs of peanut butter on the cones and hang with yarn or string from a tree branch outside your window.

3. Pine cones have nice fat bodies that can easily be transformed into animals and people. Cut ears and eyes from construction paper—use pipe cleaners for limbs and tails.

Pine-cone Owl

MATERIALS:
 1 nice fat pine cone
 glue stick
 cardboard
 construction paper
 scissors

Make sure you get a pine cone that will "stand up" on its base when the owl's feet are glued to the bottom of the cone.

Use the pattern in the diagram below as a guide for cutting 2 large owl feet out of the cardboard. Put the feet on a flat place and cover them heavily with glue. Then press the pine cone firmly onto the feet and hold in place for a few minutes until the cone is stuck.

To make wide eyes for the owl, cut 2 large circles out of the construction paper. On each eye draw another circle and color it in. Glue the circles onto the pine cone near the top.

Finish off the owl with wings cut out of construction paper. Draw lines on the wings to indicate feathers, and glue the wings to the sides of the cone.

Twig Wigwam

MATERIALS:
 several twigs about the same diameter, broken into 12″ lengths
 construction paper
 crayons or Magic Markers
 glue stick
 Scotch tape
 scissors

Use a whole sheet of 8½″ × 11″ construction paper to make the wigwam cover. Draw a half

circle on the paper and cut it out. Decorate it with Indian designs.

For each wigwam, stand 3 twigs together. Tie them at the top with yarn or Scotch tape.

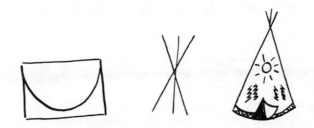

Wrap the wigwam cover around the twigs to make a cone. Overlap the edges and Scotch tape. Cut a flap for a door in the wigwam, and it is ready to take its place in an Indian village.

Pumpkin Hunt

Selecting the perfect pumpkins for Hallowe'en jack-o'-lanterns can stimulate a special outing. Find a pick-your-own patch if you can; take a drive in the country to inspect farmers' stands; or pick them up at your local market. But do let the kids have the fun of choosing their own pumpkins to carve. Save one to make a basket that can center the table at Hallowe'en or Thanksgiving.

Pumpkin Basket

MATERIALS:
 medium-sized pumpkin
 Magic Markers
 knife
 plastic wrap
 fresh fruit

With a Magic Marker, mark the outline of the handle and top of the basket on the pumpkin shell. Then cut away the unwanted portion of the pumpkin, leaving the basket and handle in one piece. Cut out the insides of the handles, and scrape the inside clean. Line the inside of the

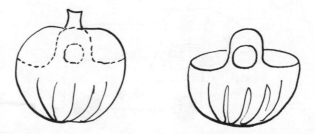

pumpkin shell with plastic wrap and fill the basket with fresh fruit.

Pumpkin Seeds

Save the seeds from carved pumpkins for a tasty snack kids can make themselves (under adult supervision, of course). Wash and dry the seeds. Then roast them in a 350° F. oven until slightly brown. Sprinkle with salt and munch, munch. Any leftover seeds can be stored in a covered glass container.

KNOW YOUR NEIGHBORHOOD

Whether you live in the city or the country, you probably have near you a firehouse, a post office, and a police station. A visit to any of these places can give you and your preschooler lots to talk about and ideas for things to do at home afterward. You can make some additions to your cereal-box village, or try some of the following projects.

At the Firehouse

Call ahead to ask the firemen when would be a convenient time for you and your preschooler to drop by. Chances are you'll find a friendly fireman who will take the time to show you around and let your child handle some of the equipment. If the firehouse has a bunkroom, ask to see that, too, so your kids get the idea of 24-hour readiness. And if the firehouse has an old-fashioned sliding pole, perhaps your fireman guide will demonstrate.

Milk-carton Fire Engine

After you get home, dig into the recycle box for an empty milk carton and help your child make his own fire engine.

MATERIALS:
    one 1-quart- or half-gallon-sized milk carton
    scissors
    construction paper—red and black
    glue stick
    black Magic Marker

Lay the milk carton on its side (the slanted end will be the front of the engine). Cut away the bottom two thirds of the side, leaving the top third for the roof of the engine's cab. Make the cab look more cablike by cutting away about 1" on the sides of the carton that are now the sides of the back of the truck (as in the picure).

Cover the carton with glued-on red construction paper. Use the black Magic Marker to draw windows on the cab. Complete the engine by cutting 4 circles from the black construction paper and gluing them on the sides of the carton for wheels.

Fire Chief Hat

Try making this simple hat as a souvenir of the visit:

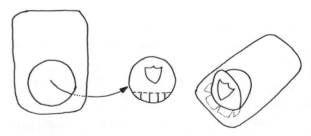

MATERIALS:
    1 sheet red construction paper, 8½" × 11"
    1 sheet yellow construction paper
    scissors
    crayon
    glue stick

To make the brim of the hat, cut around the

corners of the sheet of red construction paper so they looked curved.

To make the crown, draw on the red paper a circle approximately 6½" in diameter and about 2" in from the front edge of the brim. Cut the circle out, leaving a hole where you will later reinsert the crown.

To decorate the hat, draw a badge on the yellow paper—about 3" tall—and cut it out.

To assemble the hat, lay the red cutout circle on a flat place and draw a straight line on it about 2" from the edge. Glue the yellow badge on the upper part of the circle above the line.

Now make tabs for the crown with 4 cuts in the part of the circle below the line. Put glue on each of the tabs, and fold the circle on the line.

Insert the crown into the hole of the brim and press down firmly on the brim so the glue on the tabs will stick. If necessary, trim off any protruding tabs.

At the Post Office

Next time you have letters to mail, take your preschooler with you to the post office and let him drop them in the letter slot. Slip in a postcard addressed to him—or help him write one himself. If he can't write, you can fill in the address—then let him glue a picture cut out of a magazine onto the message space. At any rate, he will enjoy making the postcard and waiting to see how long it takes for the mail carrier to bring it back to your house!

All kids love to send and get mail. Older children get a kick out of making, addressing, and mailing birthday party invitations and cards for birthdays, Valentine's Day, Christmas, and other holidays.

Name and Address

Mailing a letter may be a good time to check to make sure your child, especially a preschooler, knows his complete name and address. If he can't write it, at least make sure he can say it clearly—in the event he should ever be lost or be asked questions to fill out a routine form at school.

You might make a large fake letter for his room—with his name and address clearly spelled out. As he learns to read, this can be a constant reminder that he does know the street where he lives.

At the same time you might ask if he knows his parents' full names and address (especially if one parent lives elsewhere). This may seem terribly obvious, but I am always surprised at how many *Romper Room*-age children are foggy about their names and addresses.

Invisible Ink

Kids who can write are intrigued by corresponding with their pals with secret messages written in invisible ink.

YOU WILL NEED:
lemon juice (½ a lemon is sufficient)
small pointed stick or toothpick for writing
paper

Dip the toothpick into the lemon juice and write a message. When the juice dries, the words will be invisible. But when the paper is held up close to a warm light bulb, the words will turn brown and magically reappear.

Kids who want to send secret messages this way should enclose directions for reading, perhaps printed at the top of the paper in pencil. If they don't, the letter will look like a blank piece of paper and may end up in a wastebasket.

Puzzle Messages

Another intriguing way to correspond is to cut up a written letter into jigsaw puzzle pieces, put the pieces in an envelope, and mail them to a friend. Puzzle letters will be easier to fit together to read if the writer writes them on construction paper or lightweight cardboard. Heart-shaped puzzles are especially fun to send on Valentine's Day with a funny greeting.

The writer can prolong the agony of the puzzle reader by sending only one or two pieces of his message at a time. Just be sure there aren't too many pieces (8 or 10 is about right); the lucky recipient may lose some before all the pieces arrive!

Postmark Map

If your family receives lots of out-of-town mail —or if you travel frequently and are in the habit of sending postcards, you can combine a kid's interest in how the mail works with a subtle lesson in geography by putting up a postmark map.

MATERIALS:
  old envelopes and postcards with canceled postmarks
  scissors
  map of the United States (or world, if you receive much foreign mail)
  glue stick

Show your child how to use the scissors to cut the postmarks off the envelopes and postcards. Help him find on the map the state from which each circle was mailed. Then he can glue the circles onto the appropriate states.

This is a good project to undertake at Christmastime when letters may be coming in from all over the country. You can make your own United States map by tracing one from an atlas. Or you can buy an inexpensive one at a stationery or school-supply store. (For a detailed map, write the National Geographic Society, 17th and "M" Streets, N.W., Washington, D.C., 20006. A U.S. map measuring about 4' by 6' costs about $6.00. Smaller world and U.S. maps are available for less.)

At the Police Station

A good time to visit the police station is when an older child has to register a two-wheeler. Again, call ahead and ask when a policeman might have a few spare minutes to talk to both the older child and to a preschooler to explain what he does.

When you get home, try making fingerprint pictures or a policeman's badge.

Fingerprint Pictures

Kids probably know from television shows that people taken into custody at police stations are usually fingerprinted. Let them make their own

fingerprints with an ink pad and paper. First, let them print the tips of each finger on each hand as in the picture at left. Draw hand outlines to show where the prints belong.

Then, they might get a kick out of making more fingerprints and embellishing them with pencil drawings.

If more than one child is fingerprinting, you can point out how different prints are. Fingerprinting is used for identifying people because no two fingerprints are ever alike. Each one is unique in the world.

Policeman's Badge

TO MAKE A SHINY BADGE, YOU WILL NEED:
   1 aluminum pie tin
   scissors
   paint or Magic Markers
   large safety pin
   tape

Draw the shape of a badge on the flat part of the pie tin. Show your child how to cut out the badge with the scissors. Use the Magic Markers or paint to put a number on the badge. Tape the pin to the badge, so the young police "person" can pin the badge on his shirt.

CHAPTER SEVEN

Weekends Are Never Long Enough

Preview:

FACTS VS. FANTASIES

SUNDAY MORNING SLEEP-IN LIST

EVERYBODY OUTINGS

BABY-SITTER BUDGET

OVERNIGHT SURVIVAL KIT

TRAVELING WITH KIDS

HOME, SWEET HOME

I DON'T KNOW A SINGLE HUMAN BEING, ESPE-cially a working parent, who doesn't tend to put off until the weekend everything that didn't get accomplished during the week. There's something about the seductive lure of unstructured time that deceives us into believing that Saturday and Sunday can be a catch-all for all the loose ends of our private lives. But too often we end up frustrated and exhausted Sunday night from failing to achieve the impossible: How can you jam into two days—Saturday errands, Sunday church, family get-togethers, activities and games for the kids, a social life for grown-up friends—and still carve out time for yourself?

You might find it helpful to tell yourself that we call Saturday and Sunday the week*end,* but those two days are also the *beginning* of the week. That break from your work routine has to sustain you and the family for another five days. It's too easy to be caught in a whirlwind of trying to do the "right thing"—from rooting for your kids' teams on Saturday to concocting an elaborate family Sunday breakfast. Why do parents who plan time to do nothing often suffer from an enormous guilt trip?

I think feeling guilty for not being perfect is ridiculous. In fact, I applaud those busy people who admit they regularly spend a whole day in bed. More than any other chapter in this book, this chapter is for parents. You can't do it all every weekend. Make choices that leave time for yourself, too.

FACTS VS. FANTASIES

You can resist going into accelerated overdrive on the weekends if you realize that every moment does not have to be planned. Slowing down the tempo of your life leaves room for spontaneity. Try to settle for having an "umbrella" idea of what you would like to have happen so that it will happen. If you are realistic about setting priorities, you won't wake up Monday morning wondering where did all the time go.

1. Don't Overschedule

Be practical in assessing how much time is really available on weekends to take care of new and unfinished business. If you count up the hours, you'll see that the notion of endless time is an illusion. At maximum, you will have thirty-two hours. But even this amount of time is misleading, since you have to spend some time eating and doing routine household chores. Suppose you counted the time this way:

    Friday evening: 6 P.M. to 10 P.M. (4 hours)
    Saturday: 8 A.M. to 10 P.M. (14 hours)
    Sunday: 8 A.M. to 10 P.M. (14 hours)

That schedule adds up to thirty-two hours. Now if you were to get up at 6 A.M. and stay up until midnight, you could squeeze out ten more hours, but who wants to? This kind of exercise is admittedly academic. But if you can be realistic about the number of hours that are actually "free" on your weekend, it might be easier to say "no," to eliminate, to not feel pressured to aim for too much.

2. Practice Time Sharing

How you divide up your weekend time obviously depends on the size of your family. Two parents with one infant don't face the logistical problems that perplex the parents of four school-age kids, each with different interests and activities. But must weekends be an endless litany of little league, soccer games, tennis matches, and gymnastics practices? I don't think so.

Even before conflicts arise, talk to your kids about time sharing. You can't be everywhere at once, and you can't do everything every weekend. A pie can only be cut into so many pieces. Kids will take your absence less personally and appreciate your presence more if you explain to them that each person will get his share, even if they have to take turns. Rotating favorites is not playing favorites; it's just plain common sense.

Each person, of course, includes each parent. When I feel pulled in too many directions, I recite as my motto: "For the good of all, everybody must get some of the goods." Divide up the time as best you can, but insist on some for yourself as well as for others. If you make your time-sharing rules clear, kids will know you expect to have some fun over the weekend, too.

3. Learn to Eliminate

Simplify your weekend expectations by shortening your list of all those things you know deep down you'll never get around to doing. If you stretch too much and try to paint the house, plant a garden, see your best friends, host a birthday party, and shop at the supermarket—all in two days—you'll be exhausted, not refreshed, on Monday morning. Try to discipline yourself to focus on one major project. Then you know you'll get that done. What progress you make on the others will feel like a bonus, not a burden.

4. Distinguish Between Rituals and Routines

When I'm hard-pressed for time on a weekend, I sometimes say to myself, "What would happen if I don't do 'X'?" That question helps me pare down my list to essentials. Most of my routine plans—shopping, gardening, cleaning—can be shifted to another day of the week, or even skipped altogether. But rituals we value—such as visiting the grandparents or our Sunday night supper with the kids—I try never to cut. I make the distinction in my mind this way. Routines keep the household running smoothly; rituals give a sense of permanence to our family life and

should be fun. When any sacred ritual turns into a profane routine, that's the time to drop it and find another.

5. Accept Inevitable Disasters

If you're away from home at work all week, don't be surprised by some kind of upsetting attention-getting behavior from the kids over the weekend. Children can sense when you're overanxious or trying to please, and are not unknown to throw a temper tantrum or start fighting among themselves at precisely the moment you're trying your best to stage something special. Reassurance of your love can somewhat quiet their rage. But I think you'll feel better if from the outset, you don't try to make up to them in two days for having been away five. Disasters happen. No more need be said. Think positively about next weekend.

SUNDAY MORNING SLEEP-IN LIST

I'm a great believer in what I call my "sanity lists"—lists not of must-do chores, but of ways everybody else at home can make me feel good.

Try my Sunday morning sleep-in scenarios, and let me know what lists you have contrived to keep your sense of humor.

Preschool "Cooks"

With foresight and preplanning on your part, even very young children with little experience in the kitchen can take charge of their own breakfast on Sunday mornings while you have a special snooze. Here's my battle plan:

On Saturday night before you go to bed, use your imagination and common sense to lay out anything and everything that is already prepackaged or preprepared by you. These goodies should not involve manipulating any electrical appliances.

1. In the refrigerator you could put:
   dishes of cottage cheese or applesauce
   glasses of prepoured juice

bowls with milk already added for cereal
buttered bread
peeled hard-boiled eggs
sliced fruit
a can of prewhipped cream

2. On the counter, you might put on a tray:
   boxes of cereal
   doughnuts—the more variety the better
   a jar of peanut butter
   crackers
   packages of dried fruit and nuts

The night before you try this the first time, you might discuss with your child the breakfast possibilities. Point out the fun of choosing. When Jenny was small, I even went to the trouble of writing her a note, and reading it to her the night before. I pasted a picture of her at the top of the paper, pasted pictures of breakfast food below, and ended with a drawing of a clock—with hands showing the time she could wake me up in the morning. Believe me, the extra time in making a game out of Sunday morning, and even the inevitable mess in the kitchen when I do get up, is well worth the luxury of the extra rest.

EVERYBODY OUTINGS

Trial and Error

Discovering the type of outing or activity that everyone enjoys may take some experimenting, especially as kids grow older and become more involved in making plans with their friends rather than with the family.

In our family something outdoorsy seems to be the answer. I enjoy tennis, jogging, biking, and hiking, and from the time my two children were small, I've slowly tried to introduce them to these sports on weekends. Since we all enjoy these activities, no one feels gypped.

But to arrive at this solution, I've done a lot of eliminating. We've tried going to plays, but the children weren't ready to sit still for dramatic theater. Movies sound like a good idea, but we can seldom all agree on the choice of a film. While fast-food restaurants don't stir up squabbles, they also are neither special nor satisfying.

Our favorite outing now is a family bike trip. We don't do this every weekend, or even every other weekend. Six times a year is more accurate. We continue to plan bike trips because they are the one activity everyone looks forward to. None of us feels forced to go or deprived of doing something else just to satisfy an obligation of "togetherness."

When you are planning a family outing, I would suggest that you don't give very young children too many choices. They just can't handle the confusion and are apt to change their minds midstream. I think you'll have better luck if you start them out on something you already enjoy. If you like going to museums, chances are your child will respond to your enthusiasm. If you drag him through a museum because you think it's good for him, he'll probably loathe every single minute.

Calculating the Cost

Many outings families would like to plan or kids dream up are frankly too expensive. Lest the children write you off as a stingy miser, you can use these occasions as opportunities for a dose of economic education. Without telling the kids about your mortgage payments and debts, you can show them what's affordable by letting them plan an outing that fits your budget.

For example, if your kids badger you about going more often to fast-food restaurants, let them know the cost is high. Next time you go, give them a budget of "X" and let them pay the bill. That helps them to understand why you may have to establish a regular rule of fast food only once a week. To reduce the cost, you can suggest they look for newspaper coupons to bring along on subsequent trips.

Or, let them plan an outing within a more general budget. For example, explain that you can allow $15 per week for family entertainment. They can spend the money any way they want, but may have to decide between doing one expensive thing or two cheapies. Depending on the size of your family, they may find the $15 could offer these choices:

    1 ball game or
    1 movie or
    1 concert (2 weeks) or

    1 theater (2 weeks) or
    1 hike (equipment, food) or
    1 boat rental or
    1 visit to a nearby town (gas and snack)

Turning over a budget to kids not only gives them a sense of what money will and will not buy, but also lets them know you're honest when you say, "I'm broke. Plan a freebie."

Freebies (or "Almost" Freebies)

Put a twist on obvious ideas. For example:

1. Try night swimming at the local "Y" or a friend's pool. Somehow swimming at night holds glamour and adventure for kids.

2. Pack the family in the car and go to a drive-in movie. Nowadays drive-in movies are a disappearing art form.

3. Duckpin bowling may not be your game, but kids love it. Everyone can handle the small lightweight balls.

4. Get your hands on a schedule of events for a local college. Tickets to games, movies, good music are usually inexpensive.

5. Find a quiet street for roller skating, or in winter, a pond for ice skating. Let the kids race if your ankles are wobbly.

6. Fly a kite at sunset.

BABY-SITTER BUDGET

Let's face it. The baby-sitter is no longer a luxury; for working parents with young children, a good reliable baby-sitter is as essential to survival as food and sleep. Whether your sitter is a neighborhood teenager who comes in while you go to a Friday night movie, or is an adult who takes care of your children eight hours a day while you are at work, she (or he) is indispensable to your peace of mind.

Most working parents count the expense of a weekday sitter as part of the cost of going to work. But if you habitually hire a sitter over the weekends, by all means include that expense into your basic budget. Many young couples feel trapped by their inability to do things spontaneously over the weekend. Arranging to have a regular responsible person on call means you have to pay the sitter whether you go out or not. But the cost is worth the sense of freedom. Nothing is more frustrating than phoning two dozen teenagers and begging them to sit so that you can accept a last-minute invitation.

Be ingenious and perhaps you won't have to spend any extra money. If you're lucky, you can call on doting grandparents or relatives. In most neighborhoods or apartment buildings you can usually find other parents with whom you can work out swaps.

Sitters as Substitutes

What can a baby-sitter do—other than just sit in the house when you are not there?

Obviously, the baby-sitter can do any household job that you make arrangements with her to have done. That's easy.

Some parents who have to be away from home a good deal of the time are fearful that the baby-sitter will replace them as a mother or father figure.

But I think you can let a baby-sitter be responsible—if, of course, you pick a responsible baby-sitter—for *anything* you have to do with your child that doesn't have to do with his feelings and his basic philosophy of life.

In other words, if you've got somebody you can trust, you can count on that baby-sitter to do errands with your child, take him to the dentist, play outdoor games, teach the letters of the alphabet, go over homework—the list is endless. If you take a little time with the sitter to discuss exactly what you have in mind—what games you think are suitable, for example—you can successfully delegate a number of things that would be fun for the child to do when you can't be there yourself.

But anything that really goes to the core of a child his fear of the dark, for instance, or a fight with a friend—you will probably want to handle. I don't think you can delegate how a child deals with other people to the baby-sitter.

But most of the other jobs don't matter—as long as they get done. If you care who your child plays with, you can leave a list. If you care how much time your child watches television, you can explain your limits to the sitter. Most people don't like to make up rules, but you can't expect a sitter to think them up. *You* have to make the rules. And then you find somebody to follow them. Let the baby-sitter carry out the plans you have organized. But when your child's feelings are involved, break all the rules and be with him to work them out yourself.

OVERNIGHT SURVIVAL KIT

The first time a child goes to someone else's house to spend the night is always the hardest. Even though he leaves home in excitement, you may get a midnight phone call hearing him say he wants to come home, or find out from him the next morning that he cried himself to sleep. On the other hand, he may announce upon his return that he had a super time and wants to sleep over all the time!

You can make initial overnights easier by making sure the surroundings are friendly, perhaps a best friend's house where he has played before during the day. One very practical reason for making contact with the parents of your child's playmates (or play group) is to be prepared when invitations for spending the night do begin.

Packing for the trip is simple. All your child needs are a sleeping bag and a knapsack. Any kind of sleeping bag will do, but if you have to buy one, look for a funny colorful bag to make these outings special. I recently saw a sleeping bag stitched up to look like a cat, complete with arms that fold over the tucked-in child.

In the knapsack let your child carry a change of clothes, pajamas, a toothbrush, and a familiar blanket or stuffed animal. If he forgets to pack the extra clothes and the toothbrush, don't fret. He probably won't use them anyway.

When it's your turn to be the host parent, don't worry if a visiting child can't go to sleep. Most doctors say children will eventually get the sleep they need. If the child seems anxious, you might suggest that he bring his toys and sleeping bag into your room. Turn on a low light and let him play quietly. Chances are you'll soon find him asleep on the floor.

Once your child is old enough (probably at least six) to enjoy the idea of overnights, you might seek out other families with whom sleepovers could be a regular baby-sitting exchange. Nothing is more fun for grown-ups than a night or weekend vacation at home without the kids, especially when you know they're having a good time elsewhere.

TRAVELING WITH KIDS

Old Suitcase Trick Number Two

When I am planning a trip with my children, I know they are bound to get restless. So I always let each one take with him a small carry-on bag which he's expected to carry himself (most obvious for airplane trips, but also useful for trips on trains and in cars). "Imagine you are going to be on a desert island for a few hours," I say. "Put in your bag some things you know you would like to have with you." The children each pack their own bags with the toys or just junk they want to take on the trip. The size of the bag keeps them from taking too much; packing it themselves teaches them to be responsible for their own entertainment.

Since food can sometimes be a problem when traveling (especially on airplanes where there's likely to be little choice of meals), I let the kids take something they know they like to eat. It could be a sandwich, a piece of fruit, cheese and crackers wrapped in foil, or even usually forbidden potato chips and candy bars. The point is that when they open the carry-on bag on the trip, they have something to look forward to. And instead of my having to worry about how we're going to get through the long hours ahead, the traveling becomes more enjoyable for all of us.

The Old Duffel-bag Caper

Into the bottom of my suitcase, whenever I travel with the kids, always goes an empty duffel bag. As dirty clothes pile up, I stuff them in the bag. On the return trip I simply check that duffel bag full of dirty laundry as an extra suitcase—and forget about it until we get home.

Think Comfort, Not Chic

Especially if you are embarking on a long trip, comfortable clothing for all of you is a must. An extra shirt or two in your carry-on bag for each child can keep the kids from getting too grubby. A box of wash-and-dry towelettes can also refresh grimy hands and faces.

If you have any room left in your carry-on bag, tuck in a few surprises to relieve boredom or crankiness. Try wrapping the surprises; undoing the packages will keep a child fascinated for a few extra peaceful minutes. Some parents take along on car trips a "grab bag." Each child can reach into the bag for a surprise at specified intervals. Then everyone can anticipate having his turn.

When you finally take off for that "dream vacation" with the children, be ready for problems

and disappointments. I learned this the hard way. One year I took my kids to a wonderful West Coast "hideout"—an old frontier hotel with saloon doors, a cowboy front porch, and old-fashioned beds. I was charmed, but much to my surprise, the kids hated the place. Why? Because there were no modern bathrooms and no television. The children had traveled for eleven hours without a gripe, and then exploded. They needed the old familiar amenities to feel comfortable in a strange place. Since that time, I've tried to let them know ahead of time what to expect.

HOME, SWEET HOME

To close this chapter on a reflective note, almost every weekend I remind myself how important it is to live in my own mind. A child can have a closed door. You can do what you want to for yourself without being neglectful. Everybody needs some quiet time. And a family can enjoy solitude together.

One of my favorite photographs in the *Family of Man* collection by Edward Steichen is a picture of a father and his young son lying foot-to-foot on a sofa reading the Sunday newspapers. Maybe that kind of intimate moment is enough for a child to know a parent thinks he's special. Although this book is crammed with projects and suggestions, I'd like to think its message is simple: avoid the artificial; do what works best for you; to enjoy being a parent means, above all, to relax.

CHAPTER EIGHT

Adventures in Art

Preview:
CREATING WITH CLAY
PAINTLESS PICTURES
PROJECTS WITH PAINT
PAPER WEAVING
EARLY-AMERICAN DOLLS

EVERY SO OFTEN YOU MAY BE LUCKY ENOUGH to find yourself with a day when you don't have to ration every minute—maybe during a week of vacation or on a lazy Sunday afternoon. That might be a good time to forget the clock and experiment with some unhurried projects that challenge your children's creativity. The art projects in this chapter, and the science projects in Chapter Nine, don't promise to diagnose talent; but they do give kids a chance to be inventive, especially if they seem to have an interest you'd like to encourage.

You don't have to be a Rembrandt or a Picasso yourself to notice whether one of your kids seems to have a knack for working with his hands or a feel for color and design. And you don't have to be a Madame Curie or a Ben Franklin to realize that some kids are more ob-

servant than others. But in the case of both art and science, a little extra time spent to nurture unusual curiosity just might open a door for a gifted child. At the very least, the more experience a child has in pursuing something he likes, the more confidence he will have in discovering for himself later on just what talents he does have.

Some preschoolers have nimble fingers as early as three; others may be seven or eight before their small hands seem coordinated to work with detail. And some very bright children just never seem comfortable at anything that requires manual dexterity. The "art" projects in this chapter are really simple crafts that can be handled by all of these kids. You can't expect masterpieces, but you can look for some decorative results that should give you both pleasure.

CREATING WITH CLAY

One of the virtues of making things from salt-dough "clay" is that you can have next-day results without having to fool with kilns or glazes. It goes without saying that the ingredients for an afternoon of this kind of clay modeling are inexpensive staples always at hand on your pantry shelf. Show the kids how easy this mixture is to work with by helping them to make the shell and stone paperweight below.

Shell and Stone Paperweight

This "sculpture" takes its shape from a paper cup. Use it as a paperweight, or display it on a shelf.

MATERIALS:
  paper cups—one for each child
  sand
  shells, small stones, buttons, etc.
  1 recipe salt-dough (see Chapter One)

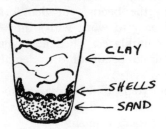

Start by putting a layer of sand in the bottom of the cup so that the cup is about ¼ full. The sand will hold steady the objects that your child will set in the clay.

Next, show your child how to stand up the stones and shells in the sand. Put them around the sides of the cup as well as in the middle so that they will show after the clay has hardened.

Now show him how to press a glob of salt-dough into the objects and sand so that the cup is firmly packed with clay. Let sit overnight or until the salt-dough has hardened.

To unveil the "sculpted" paperweight, cut away the paper cup and the shells and stones will be mounted on a base of clay. To avoid mess, do the cutting over a piece of newspaper to catch the sand—which will, of course, fall away.

NOTE: Although they are a bit harder to cut, clear plastic cups work well for this project, too, because the kids can see how the clay presses into the objects to make the sculpture.

Mexican Posado

Common in Mexico at Christmastime are *posado* processions of small animal figures. Using salt-dough, show your child how to make a small burro and then encourage him to shape more animals for his own *posado*.

MATERIALS:

1 recipe salt-dough clay
waxed paper—to place dough on
lots of wet and dry towels to avoid mess
Magic Markers

Ambitious kids may want to try to make simple people figures, too. Peasants with long skirts and trousers work best so that you don't have to worry about spindly arms and legs breaking. Arms can be modeled close to the body.

After your child has completed his figures, let them sit overnight to harden. Then he can color and decorate them with Magic Markers—and arrange them in a procession.

Noah's Ark

An ongoing salt-dough clay project could be the making of pairs of animals for your child's own Noah's Ark. He can let his imagination go wild—starting with simple ducks and rabbits, trying giraffes, crocodiles, or even long slimy worms and snakes. Perhaps he would even like to invent some never-before-seen creatures of his own. This menagerie can be decorated with Magic Markers—as was the Mexican *posado*—poster paints, or even egg paint made at home according to the directions that follow.

For a simple ark, make a cereal-box shed (see Chapter Four) and place it on a large box lid. Then the animals can be arranged on the "lid" deck.

Egg Paint

This recipe is useful to fall back on when you need only a few colors (red and green for Christmas decorating, for example). Unless you want to use up a lot of egg yolks, I think poster paints or Magic Markers are easier to work with.

MATERIALS:

1 egg yolk (enough for 2 colors)
water
food coloring
cup and spoon for mixing

Separate the egg yolk into 2 equal parts, and put each part in a cup. Add enough water to each cup to give the yolk a paintlike consistency (it will be sticky). To each cup, add a few drops of food coloring and mix with the spoon. Dip a brush into the "paint" and use to color objects made from salt-dough clay.

Clay Beads

Making original jewelry can be a continuing hobby if your kids enjoy stringing this necklace.

MATERIALS:

1 recipe salt-dough clay
food coloring
toothpicks
dental floss

While you are mixing the clay, add a few drops of food coloring. For a multicolored necklace, separate the clay into different dishes and color each one separately.

Now show your child how to roll lumps of the clay into small bead-size balls. Pierce each ball through the middle with a toothpick; then put the balls aside to dry for at least a day.

To string the beads, cut dental floss (very strong and easy to work with) into lengths for bracelets or necklaces. Then help your child to string the dried beads on the dental floss (no needle is necessary).

If you and your child are making the beads for gifts, don't forget that bead necklaces are popular with both men and women.

PAINTLESS PICTURES

Experimenting with materials other than paint can help to give a child a feeling for texture as well as design. Get out the old reliable glue stick and show your preschooler how easy it is to make shapes with natural materials—such as salt, sand, and seeds. Then the two of you may want to scrounge around the house for buttons, bits of fabric, scraps of paper—anything glueable —to construct more elaborate collages.

Salt, Sand, and Seed Painting

FOR EACH OF THESE METHODS, YOU WILL NEED:

glue stick
construction paper or lightweight cardboard
paper cups or bowls to hold the salt, sand, or seeds
spoon
food coloring (for salt and sand)
Magic Markers (for seeds)

The general procedure is the same for all three materials. Show your child how to draw a picture or a shape on the construction paper with a glue stick. Start with something recognizable and easy —such as a flower or a house. Then use the spoon to sprinkle different bits of colored sand or salt or different kinds of seeds on sections of the picture. Stand up the piece of paper and tap off the excess material.

To color the salt or sand, place small amounts in different paper cups and tint with a few drops of food coloring. Stir to mix thoroughly. When "painting," apply one color at a time and shake off the excess before using another color. For a "salt" daisy, for example, start with a yellow center—then apply white salt for petals, green salt for stem and leaves. Stand up the finished painting to let it dry.

Packages of bird seed or sunflower seeds make intriguing patterns. Even a package of small dried beans will work. For a "seed" daisy, for example, place small seeds in the center, larger seeds on the petals. Draw in the green leaves and stem with Magic Markers for a contrast in color.

After the kids have gotten the knack of "painting" something they recognize, you might suggest they try some free-form designs: "ribbons" of different colors of sand or salt, for example, or "mosaics" of sand. The only limits to the kinds of shapes they can dream up are patience and imagination.

Designs with Toothpicks, Straws, and Twigs

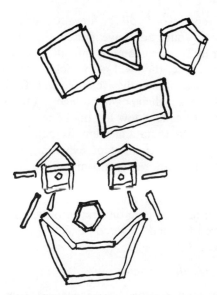

A box of toothpicks, a box of straws, a handful of twigs gathered on a walk—all of these can be inspirations for designs. For pictures with these materials, you will need:

glue stick
scissors
construction paper
short lengths of string (optional)

Let the kids fiddle with the toothpicks or straws at first to see how many shapes they can make. They can break the toothpicks or cut the straws to make shorter lines if they like. Suggest something easy, like a flag or a house—or even a geometric shape like a triangle or a square.

When they have made a design they are especially fond of, show them how to place the toothpicks or the straws on a piece of construction paper and then glue the pieces in place. Use the lengths of string to add circular shapes, such as wheels for a truck, or the head of a straw "person."

Twigs, of course, do not have straight edges, but can be broken to make rustic lines for a "log cabin" house or a miniature "tree."

As with the salt, sand, and seeds, kids who enjoy working with these different kinds of sticks can go on to compose free-form designs: thick and thin patches of toothpicks, for example, or fans and stars of straws. The irregularities in twig shapes lend themselves to many ideas.

Collages

The French word *collage* literally means "pasting." Once your kids have gotten the idea that they can make pictures by gluing all kinds of materials to a base, they will get a kick out of seeing what unusual items they can collect from the house to make their own collages. You might even want to take a few art books out of the library to show them that famous painters—like Picasso—were often fond of experimenting with collages. Try working with some of the materials below individually at first. Then you can progress to combining them and to figuring out which items you have to glue on first in order to create the desired finished "layered" effect.

Button People

Surely your button box can yield some interesting "faces" for button people. The ones with two holes—for eyes—are the most realistic, but any round button will do. You will need:

> buttons
> construction paper
> glue stick
> Magic Markers or crayons

Start with a large button and glue it on the paper. Then let your child use his imagination and the crayons to draw the rest of the figure. Several different kinds of buttons glued onto a piece of paper can add to the "personalities" of the faces of a family of button people.

(Buttons, of course, can be used in all kinds of designs—as the centers of flowers, for example, or as wheels for vehicles. If your child likes the button people, let him see what else he can make from buttons—including free-form designs.)

Patchwork Buildings

You can use leftover pieces of colored construction paper, bits of fabric from your sewing basket, or clippings from magazines and newspapers to make a variety of building shapes. These make interesting patterns in themselves, or can be used as the background for a layered collage. You will need:

> scraps of fabric or paper
> Magic Marker or pencil
> scissors
> construction paper or cardboard
> glue stick

If your child is confident and adept with scissors, he can cut building shapes directly from the fabric or paper. If he's shaky, help him draw an outline on the material first as a cutting line. Start him out on a patchwork house—cutting different materials for the basic square shape, the roof, the chimney, the windows, the doors, window boxes, and so on. Then show him how to glue the pieces on the paper one at a time—starting with the basic box shape and adding the other pieces to it.

After kids have made one house, they usually catch on quickly to making a whole row of build-

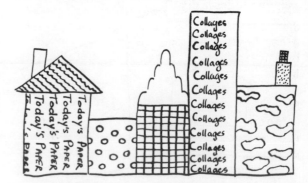

ings—either a street scene or a city skyline. Remind them to keep the shapes simple. The whole idea is to use as many different patterned pieces as possible—to create a lively contrast between simple building shapes and textured designs.

Shoe-box Lid Specials

Once your child has worked with all of these various materials, he'll find it easy to combine them in his own original collage. For an instantly "framed" picture, suggest he arrange his creation on the inside of a shoe-box lid. You'll probably have to help him go through all the steps of assembling the pieces in order.

To make a simple scene from fabric scraps, buttons, and cotton, for example, he should start with the fabric, cutting out his buildings and arranging them on the lid. He can glue them in place if he likes, but some kids like to wait until they have the whole picture assembled before doing any gluing.

After the buildings are situated, he can place the buttons, leaving room to draw in bodies. Finally, he can put cotton in the sky for clouds.

It's probably easiest for a young child to glue each of these materials on a different part of the lid, but older youngsters may want to experiment with layering the materials for a richer effect that gives more depth and texture to the picture.

Collages have infinite possibilities for stretching kids' imaginations and for using up leftover materials. Let your child try an aquarium, for example. Line the inside of a shoe-box lid with glued-on blue paper, cut out silver fish from aluminum foil and colored seahorses from construction paper and fabric, glue on button sea flowers and blades of real grass. To give the effect of water, you can even cover the entire creation with a piece of plastic wrap, gluing the edges to the edges of the lid.

For holidays, you can make cotton Easter Bunny scenes or rows of green Christmas trees, decorated with glued-on oddments for ornaments. Birthdays can inspire personalized greeting card pictures, designed to depict something special about the recipient.

As children become older, they may enjoy making collages with remnants of a special event, much as some families keep scrapbooks. Cut-up brochures, tickets, and photos help remember a trip; pressed flowers, ribbons, certificates commemorate school parties and awards.

PROJECTS WITH PAINT

Painting does not have to be messy if you take a few simple precautions. Protect the floor with newspapers and cover your child with a smock (a man's old shirt is dandy). All of these projects can be done on a kitchen table, but an easel, if you have one, makes brushwork easier. A child-sized easel (preferably with one side of chalkboard) is one of the few things I would suggest that you consider buying—perhaps picking one up at a neighborhood garage sale. A child who likes to draw and paint will find an easel useful almost every day.

To improvise a simple easel, try this one made from a grocery box.

Easy Easel

MATERIALS:
   a large grocery box (at least 24″ square)
   scissors or X-acto knife

You can do the cutting while your child watches. Stand the grocery box on end and cut in half diagonally—from corner to corner.

You will have 2 triangles. Since grocery boxes usually have cut lids, use the half that hasn't been cut for your easel. Turn the cut side down and you have a slanted-top easel to place on

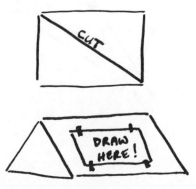

your kitchen table. Attach paper with masking tape or thumbtacks, and let your young Cézanne go to work.

Muffin-tin Palette

Premixed poster paints are the easiest and least messy to work with. If you don't want to fool with mixing colors, buy eight colors—red, yellow, blue, green, orange, purple, brown, and black—preferably in small bottles (which are less likely to spill). If you are working on a table, steady the paintpots, by placing them in the cups of a 12-cup muffin tin. Paper cupcake liners or aluminum foil will help to keep paint off the tin, but the tin makes such a handy place to store the paints (with lids on tight) that I almost think it's worth sacrificing an extra one to your home "studio."

If you have several kids—or if you want to try mixing colors—buy the big sizes of poster paints (red, yellow, blue, and black will suffice) and pour a small amount of each color into paper cups that will fit in the muffin tin. Fill the rest of the tin with empty paper cups for mixing colors —as an oil painter would do on a palette. One cup should contain water to help with the mixing.

Tips on Brushes

To avoid confusion, use one kind of brush with very young children. For *Romper Room* projects, we use a flat easel brush that is ½″ wide. You can buy these at your local art store. Since they are not very expensive, I would suggest that you purchase at least 2 for each child.

Rainbow Colors

Your child can have fun learning to mix his own colors when you show him how. With only red, yellow, and blue he can make the stripes of a rainbow.

Before tackling an arched rainbow, try a straight one.

Starting at the top of a piece of paper, paint a wide red stripe. Below it paint a second red stripe. Then, paint yellow on top of the second red stripe. Magic! An orange stripe appears.

Proceed as in the diagram below. Paint 2 yellow stripes next, and to the second add blue to make green. Finally, paint 2 blue stripes, and to the second add red to make purple.

RED
RED + YELLOW = ORANGE
YELLOW
YELLOW + BLUE = GREEN
BLUE
BLUE + RED = PURPLE

Once your child has the idea of how the colors mix, he can try an arched rainbow and even add a pot of gold at the bottom.

Rainbow Fruit

This color exercise can be a game you play together. You will need a pencil or crayon; your child will need red, yellow, and blue paint, a brush, and paper.

First, draw a large circle on the paper and put a stem and leaves on the top. Then ask your

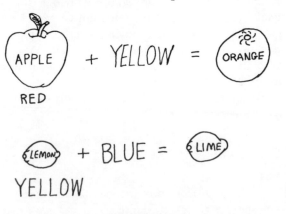

child to paint it red. It's an apple, of course. What happens when you ask him to put yellow paint on the apple? It becomes an orange.

Now draw a smaller circle and ask him to paint it yellow. It's a lemon, but when he adds blue, it becomes a lime.

Draw an even smaller circle and have him paint it blue to become a blueberry. When he adds red, it's a tiny grape.

Finally, draw a bowl with several circles above it. When the circles are painted red, you have a bowl of cherries. When your child adds blue, he has a bunch of grapes.

CHERRIES

RED + BLUE =

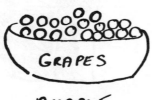

GRAPES

PURPLE

If your kids enjoy mixing their own colors, you might raid your refrigerator and vegetable bin for real-life models. What colors would he need, for example, to paint a carrot? An eggplant? A green pepper? Older kids could even try painting a bowl filled with different kinds of fruit and vegetables—either made up out of their heads or a still life which they can arrange for themselves.

Four Special Effects

Artists have always invented special techniques to give their work original touches by using instruments other than their brushes. See what your child can do with a toothbrush, a sponge, a straw, or wax paper.

Toothbrush Spatter Paint
MATERIALS:
    old toothbrush
    top of a round ice cream carton (quart-sized or larger)
    piece of window screen

    masking tape
    heavy shears (to cut screen)

An adult should assemble the spattering frame; then children can take over with toothbrushes, paper, and paint.

Cut the screen to fit the top of the ice cream carton. Attach it to the carton with masking tape, making sure any ragged edges of screen are carefully covered.

To spatter paint, place the screened carton top over a piece of paper. Then show your child how to dip an old toothbrush into paint and then rub the bristles across the screen. Spatter marks will be on the paper.

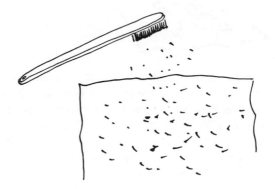

A child who becomes comfortable with this technique might want to make a "starry night" picture using only spatter paint. Use a dark piece of construction paper, navy or black, for a night background. Then spatter white and yellow "stars" on the paper.

Sponge Painting
MATERIALS:
    a sponge (this can be an old worn out sponge cut into pieces that are easy to hold)
    1 sheet of white paper
    1 sheet of colored paper
    poster paints
    brush

With the brush, put 3 or 4 large colored splotches of paint on the colored sheet of paper.

Then dip the sponge into the different colors, one at a time. Start with red, for example, and sweep and twist the sponge over the sheet of white paper. Repeat with yellow and blue.

Straw Painting

MATERIALS:

   2 or 3 drinking straws
   poster paints
   paper
   brush

With the brush, make little pools of paint on the paper. Then show your child how to hold a straw several inches from the little pools and to blow gently through the straw. The paint will blow in the direction in which he points the straw and will make fascinating designs.

Wax-paper Painting

MATERIALS:

   1 sheet of wax paper
   1 sheet of plain white paper
   pencil
   poster paints
   brush

Help your child to place the wax paper on top of the plain paper (works best if they are the same size). Then let him draw a picture or a design on the wax paper with the pencil. Tell him to press hard so that the wax lines will go through to the paper underneath. Then remove the wax paper, and let him paint the plain paper. The wax lines will resist the paint to leave the outline of the picture he drew.

PAPER WEAVING

To show kids how fabrics are made, try this simple place mat and wall hanging. Both make nice gifts, especially for an older person.

Place Mat

For a practice run, try this first with standard-sized sheets of construction paper, 8½″ × 11″. You will end up with a small child-sized mat. For a gift set of 2 or 4 mats for grown-ups, I suggest you use larger paper. You and your child can select size and colors as part of the planning for that project.

MATERIALS:

   2 sheets of construction paper in contrasting
      colors
   ruler and pencil
   scissors
   glue stick

Use the ruler to draw a straight line approximately 2″ in from the shorter edge of one sheet of the construction paper. Then cut the same sheet of construction paper into 10 strips about 1″ wide, but only up to the ruled line. (You can draw cutting lines on first with the ruler to make it easier.) Note that you will be cutting the long way.

Next, cut the other sheet of construction paper into 10 strips, this time cutting all the way through. With this sheet, cut the strips the short way—so that they can be woven into the other sheet.

Now, take one of the short strips of paper and show your child how to weave it through the long strips on the other sheet of paper, going over and under, over and under, just as people weave thread into cloth on a loom. Push the first strip all the way over to the ruled edge of the weaving sheet so that it fits tightly.

With the second strip, explain carefully that if

you began on the overside with the first strip, then you have to begin on the underside with the second strip. Again, weave the strip over and under, over and under, and push it over next to the first one so that it fits tightly. This procedure is more complicated for some preschoolers than it sounds, but by the time they have completed weaving all of the strips to finish the place mat and can see the checkerboard of colors, they usually have the idea down pat. Finish off the mat by gluing the edges on the three "fringed" sides.

Wall Hanging

Older children can construct the cardboard "loom" on which this hanging is made, but a grown-up will have to do the preliminaries for a preschooler. You will be wrapping string tightly on a piece of cardboard so that kids can then "weave" different materials in and out of the string to create a very individual and decorative hanging. This is a good project to make use of objects collected on a walk—feathers, leaves, or grass—or leftover scraps of yarn, paper, and fabric in your "make-it" drawer.

MATERIALS:
   a rectangular piece of heavy cardboard 3"
   × 5" (you can make this any size, but a
   small one is easiest to start with)

scissors
a 2′ length of string
a variety of materials for weaving: grass, straw, feathers, sticks, yarn, narrow strips of construction paper, etc.
2 popsicle sticks

Prepare the cardboard rectangle by "fringing" the top and bottom, cutting slits ¼″–½″ long. Make the string base by looping one end of the string around the first fringe slit at the top of the rectangle; then bring the string down and loop in underneath the second fringe on the bottom. Bring the string up and loop it behind the third fringe on the top. Continue in this manner until you have used all the fringes. You have made a "warp thread" to be used as the basis for weaving.

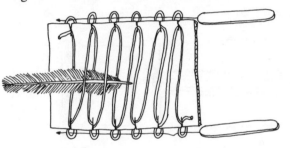

Now let the kids go to work. Show them how to take one of the materials for weaving—the feathers or grass or paper—and tuck it over and under the string base. Repeat with the other materials. You don't have to push each one to the edge of the "warp" as you did with the paper place mat, but it might be easier to do so. Aim to incorporate as many different materials as possible for an interesting rough texture.

When the entire rectangle is filled, show the kids how to insert the 2 popsicle sticks in the loops at the top and bottom so that they can hang their "creations" on the wall.

EARLY-AMERICAN DOLLS

Children growing up in colonial America often made dolls from whatever they could find among household staples. Leftover knitting yarn was popular—as were dried apples and cornhusks scrounged from the pantry. Let your kids see what they can create with these same materials in the nineteen-eighties.

Yarn Dolls

Small yarn dolls may ride in toy trucks, live in dollhouses, or even be worn as decorations on coat lapels.

MATERIALS:

a cardboard rectangle, 2″ wide and 3½″ long
cotton or wool yarn
scissors

To make the doll's body, wind the yarn the long way around the piece of cardboard until you have a fat roll (about 15 times makes a workable doll). Tie the loops together at the top of the cardboard with another small piece of yarn. Slip the loops off the card. About 1″ from the top, tie a piece of yarn around all the loops to form a head.

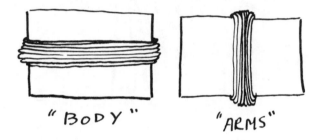

" BODY "   "ARMS"

To make the doll's arms, wind yarn around the short length of the card (about 6 times around will do). Tie loops at both ends with pieces of yarn, and slip the loops off the card.

Divide the "body" yarn loops below the head and tuck in the "arm" loops horizontally. Tie the body yarn beneath the arm loops to form the waist.

To make a girl doll, cut the loops at the bottom of the body yarn to make a fringed skirt. To make a boy doll, divide the body yarn below the waist into "legs," and tie each section at the bottom.

To make faces on the dolls, a grown-up can sew on button or yarn features.

Cornhusk Dolls

Cornhusk dolls were favorites of Indian children. They can be made with dried or green husks at any time of year when corn is available, but are especially fun to try after a summer corn

feast or as decorations for a Thanksgiving dinner table. A grown-up must help, but the procedure is not too different from making the simpler yarn dolls.

MATERIALS:

cornhusks—6″ long or longer, if you can find them
cornsilk
string
scissors
poster paints or Magic Markers

Soft husks are best for making dolls. Green ones (the inner husks are softer) can be used as is, but dried ones should be softened in warm soapy water. Soak the dried husks for about an hour until they are soft and almost transparent. Blot them well, and keep them damp while you are working by covering them with a wet cloth.

To make the doll's body, tie 4 smooth pieces of husk together at the center with a piece of string. You will have something that looks like a bow tie.

Use rolled pieces of husk or a small stone to stuff the doll's head. Over the stuffing, fold down smoothly the ends of the already tied body. Tie underneath to form the head and the neck.

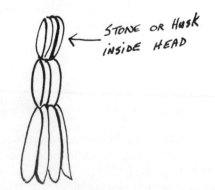

← STONE OR HUSK INSIDE HEAD

To make the arms, roll pieces of husk length-wise and tie at the ends for wrists (roll over a green twig to make them sturdier). Then place the arms between the layers of husk beneath the head. Tie the doll at the waist to hold the arms in place.

To make a girl doll, add a bodice. Use 2 narrow lengths of husks, and crisscross them at the front and back across the doll's shoulders. Tie the bodice in place at the waist. To make a fuller skirt, use 2 or more wide lengths of husk. Tie them securely at the waist of the doll as though the skirt will be upside down (the short ends of the husks will be just below the waistline, the long lengths up over the doll's head). Fold the skirt down carefully so that all the tied parts are now underneath the skirt at the waistline.

To make a boy doll, slit husks vertically from

slightly below the waist to the bottom. Tie the ends to form pants.

To make hair for both dolls, glue on cornsilk. Paint on facial features and clothes with poster paints or Magic Markers.

CHAPTER NINE

Escapades in Science

Preview:

CLOSE ENCOUNTERS

SHARPENING THE SENSES

INVENTOR'S WORKSHOP

"MAGIC" WITH WATER AND AIR

MEASURES

STOPPING TO LOOK AT THINGS IN NATURE closely and making note of our observations are the first steps in the scientific method. Preschoolers can be encouraged in this direction by taking advantage of their instinctive curiosity about the world around them. You don't even have to mention the word "science" to enjoy any of the following activities; all the projects aim to do is to capitalize on the natural inquisitiveness of the very young. Whatever "formal learning" takes place may be incidental; more important is that kids who have fun focusing on their environment may be laying a foundation for further explorations.

CLOSE ENCOUNTERS

Leaf Rubbings

Examining a leaf up close is always interesting, but making a rubbing can emphasize its distinctive shape and features. You might try this with several different leaves picked up on a walk in the park.

MATERIALS:
   leaves of various sizes
   2 sheets of lightweight paper (typing paper, for example)
   crayons

Show your child how to place a leaf between the 2 sheets of paper. Then let him rub a crayon over the top sheet of paper. As he colors, an imprint of the leaf and its veins will appear. Suggest he do the same leaf in several colors to see which shows the leaf best. If he does all of these on one large sheet of paper, he will end up with an attractive design picture.

Another way to have fun with leaf rubbings is to purposely collect leaves from your own yard and to plan a sheet of rubbings titled "My Garden."

Sunflower Seeds

MATERIALS:
   sunflower seeds
   potting soil or back-yard dirt
   bottom half of milk carton or a flowerpot
   water

The only reason for making a production out of this very simple procedure is to emphasize to your child that this is *his* plant which *he* will be watching and making notes on once a week.

Sunflower seeds are, of course, very popular with birds. One reason for starting them in a pot is to keep the birds from eating them before the plant has had a chance to sprout. When the plant is large enough, you can put it into the ground outdoors. Then the birds will be welcome.

A preschooler can do all the planting. Let him fill the milk carton or pot with dirt, advising him to leave about an inch at the top for watering. Then show him how to use his index finger to poke holes in the soil for the seeds. He should plant several seeds at a depth of about ½″—probably close in length to the end joint on his index finger (a grown-up's is about 1″ long). After he has pressed the seeds into the dirt, he should water them gently and place the pot in a warm, sunny window.

In about one month, the sunflowers should be transplanted outdoors. In about two months, your child can expect large flowers.

Parts of a Flower

Growing his own flowers may make a child more curious about just how blossoms are put together. Spring tulips and daffodils, summer daisies and day lilies, are all big enough to show him easily the three main parts of a flower.

Try a showy tulip for a mini-lesson in botany. (Don't worry about the scientific names—kids get a kick out of just hearing them. Even if they forget the exact words, they will grasp the main idea of examining something closely to understand it.) Start with the petals, the bright pretty part of the flower. A tulip doesn't have as many petals as a daisy, but in both cases, the petals protect the inside of the flower where seeds will be made. On any flower, all of the petals together are called the corolla.

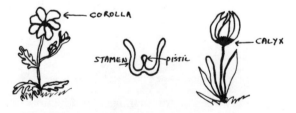

Inside the tulip, look at the long skinny parts —called the stamen. The one in the middle is called the pistil. These parts make the dusty yellow-looking pollen that is blown by the wind to other flowers to make seeds.

Finally, look at the top of the stem underneath the blossom. The parts that look like green leaves are what's left of the bud—the calyx. When the plant was too young to open up, the calyx leaves covered and protected the growing flower. When the flower was ready to bloom, the calyx spread apart—letting us see the tulip.

On your next walk through a flower garden, perhaps your child will notice that all flowers have these three parts even though they may look slightly different in different blossoms.

Move Your Own Mountains

A trip to the beach or the mountains or even a scenic television show can be the inspiration for showing your child how to make his own land formations.

MATERIALS:
    large baking pan
    small rocks for shorelines
    larger rocks for mountains
    sand for topsoil and beaches

In the bottom of the pan let your child place a number of small rocks. Gravel or small pebbles are ideal if you have them. You can tell him that the center of the earth is made of very hot rock. Then let him place a layer of sand over the pebbles for topsoil.

Now the fun begins. Let him use his imagination in adding big rocks for mountains, scooping out the pebbles for a make-believe lake, shoving some of the sand and pebbles aside for a valley. He can put an edge around the edge of the lake for a beach and add rocks for boulders on the mountains.

The idea is to make a geographical scene while suggesting that the earth as we know it is made of layers of rock and sand that have shifted through time to make mountains, valleys, lakes, and streams.

Magnifying Cup

Preschoolers can easily make their own magnifying glasses out of paper cups to take a closer look at live creatures—ants, lady bugs, or grasshoppers, for example.

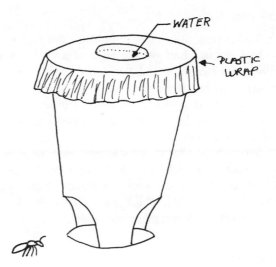

MATERIALS:
    paper cup
    scissors
    plastic wrap
    rubber band
    water
    live creatures (ants, lady bugs, etc.)

First, cut 3 holes around the base of the cup, spacing them as evenly as possible. Do not cut the bottom of the cup.

Then place plastic wrap over the top of the cup and secure it with a rubber band.

Gently push the plastic wrap in the center so that it has a slightly caved-in appearance.

Now pour water into the concave portion of the plastic wrap.

Finally, place one of the ants in the bottom of the cup and take a look. The water acts as a magnifier for the creatures in the cup. Kids will love to look at insects this way.

SHARPENING THE SENSES

Here are a few activities for the oft-neglected senses of touch and sound. (Cooking seems to take care of smell and taste, and observation and painting projects rely principally on sight.)

"Touch-me" Book

Rough, smooth, sticky, and soft—you will be making a page for each of these textures.

MATERIALS:
    6 pieces construction paper (2 for covers, 4 for pages)
    2 pieces of yarn 6″ long
    scissors
    assortment of "touch-me" articles

rough: sand, old nubby washcloths, corrugated cardboard, sandpaper, a walnut shell, emery board, steel wool, etc.
smooth: scraps of velvet, silk, felt; piece of wood; piece of paper; plastic chip
sticky: cellophane tape, lollipop, bubble gum, Velcro strip
soft: feather, cotton ball, foam rubber, fur rabbit's foot

Mix up the different textured articles on a tray or table top so the kids will have to pick them out when the time comes.

Start with "rough." Write the word on the top of a piece of construction paper and ask the kids to find rough articles from those on the table to paste on that sheet. Do the same with the other touch words—making a page for "smooth," a page for "sticky," and a page for "soft."

Complete the book by using the 2 other pieces of paper for a cover and a back. Poke 2 holes through all the sheets and tie together with the yarn. Write "Touch Me" on the front cover of the book for a title.

Singing Ruler

To make a ruler "sing," hold a ruler so that it is half on and half off the edge of a table. Bend down the free half and let it go. The "hum," of course, comes from the vibration—the basis of the sound of every musical instrument. After you've shown them how, kids can easily make the ruler sing themselves.

Show them also that by letting more or less of the ruler stick out beyond the edge of the table, they can change the sound it makes. You might explain to an older child that a guitar works on essentially the same principle.

Hummer

This simple vibrating musical instrument is made from an empty paper tube.

MATERIALS:
   paper tube (toilet-tissue roll or paper-towel tube)
   wax paper
   rubber band
   crayons or Magic Markers
   scissors

Show the kids how to cut out a circle of waxed paper larger than the end of the paper tube. Use the crayons or Magic Markers to decorate the tube with designs. Complete the tube by putting the waxed paper circle over one end and securing it with a rubber band.

When kids sing "o-o-o-o" into the open end of the tube, they can hear it hum. The vibrating paper creates the sound.

Milk-carton String Duo

Add these instruments to your Recycle Rhythm Band for a jazzy sound.

MATERIALS:
   2 empty milk cartons (quart size)
   scissors
   skinny rubber band
   wide flat rubber band
   pencil

In each of the milk cartons, cut a big window in one side. Over one of the windows, stretch the skinny rubber band. Over the other carton, stretch the wide flat rubber band.

It's easy for kids to hear the difference in sound when they pluck the skinny "string" and then the flat "string." They can also easily see the strings vibrating, just as strings do on violins and bass fiddles.

For another variation in sound, insert the pencil under the stretched rubber band on one of the milk cartons. Now when the kids pluck the rubber band, they will hear different "notes." Let them try stretching the rubber band even more by pulling the pencil toward them for even more sounds. With practice in these different techniques, kids can make the music of the milk-carton string duo an essential element in their homemade band.

INVENTOR'S WORKSHOP

You can make these in your basement "lab" if it makes you feel more like you are cultivating a young Edison, but otherwise, the good old kitchen table will do nicely.

Telephone

FOR A SIMPLE TOY TELEPHONE ALL YOU NEED ARE:
   2 paper cups

pencil or scissors

a long piece of strong thread (at least 3 yards)

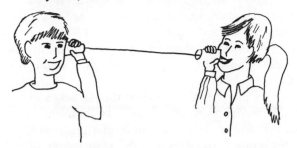

Let your child use the pencil or scissors to poke a very small hole in the bottom of each cup. Pull the thread through the holes and knot it firmly inside each cup.

One person holds a cup over his ear. The other person stretches the thread straight and talks into the other cup.

(I've suggested a 3-yard length of thread, but you can vary this according to the size of the room in which the children are playing. Just remember two criteria: the thread must be taut for the telephone to work; the thread must be long enough so that the children can't hear each other talking except over the "telephone.")

Compass

Before you show your child how to make his own compass, let him play with magnets for a while so he can see how they work. Most kids find magnets fascinating, almost magical. Explain that magnets can be found in nature (the poles) and can also be man-made.

To demonstrate how magnets work, try experimenting with a box of paper clips. Kids can have a grand time holding the magnets so that the paper clips will jump to them.

A compass works in a similar manner. A magnetized needle will always point north toward the natural magnet of the north pole, helping explorers to check their direction.

TO MAKE YOUR OWN COMPASS, YOU WILL NEED:

a magnet

a large needle

a bottle cork

water in a small container (to float the cork)

First, magnetize the compass needle by rubbing it across the magnet about a hundred times, always moving it in the same direction.

Then, push the needle into the cork. When you float the cork in the water, the needle will always point in the same direction, toward the north pole. Let the kids move the cork around to demonstrate the power of a compass.

"MAGIC" WITH WATER AND AIR

I think these work best if you don't announce that they are experiments, but perform them as "tricks" when an occasion arises. Working in the kitchen often provides a moment to demonstrate the buoyancy of eggs or wearing a sweater on a cold day gives a chance to show static electricity. Once your child's curiosity has been aroused about why these things happen, you can then set up the experiments more scientifically and give

him a chance to ask all the questions he wants to.

Chase the Pepper

This kind of "magic" demonstrates one of the properties of water—an invisible skin on the surface that pulls. The pull is strongest, as this "trick" shows, when the water is clear.

MATERIALS:

pie plate half full of water
pepper shaker
piece of wet soap
¼ cup sugar

Ask your child to sprinkle some pepper over the water and describe what happens (the pepper will scatter itself on the water's surface). To "chase" the pepper, dip the wet soap into the water on one side of the pie plate (the pepper will "run" away from the soapy water to the clear water). To "chase" the pepper back from whence it came, sprinkle the sugar into the soapy water (when the suds dissolve, the pepper will move back into the clear water).

After you have chased the pepper, you can explain that the soap suds stay on the water's surface, thus weakening the pull of the water's "skin." The sugar, on the other hand, dissolves almost immediately, and so doesn't dilute the strength of the surface pull.

Intelligent Eggs

Next time you are about to scramble eggs, have a little fun with the raw eggs before you crack them. This "trick" demonstrates another property of water—buoyancy.

MATERIALS:

2 large glasses of water (each large enough to hold an egg)
2 heaping tablespoons of salt

2 uncooked eggs
Magic Marker

While your child watches, draw with the Magic Marker a face on each egg—one sad, and one happy. The "sad" egg, you can explain mysteriously, will sink when you put him in a glass of water. The "happy" egg, on the other hand, will float.

Now put the salt in one of the glasses, and stir until it dissolves. The salt, like that in ocean water, will make the water in that glass push up with more force than will the plain water in the other glass. Put the "sad" egg in the plain water and he will sink. The "happy" egg, of course, will swim smugly in the salt water. Save any scientific explanations until after you've demonstrated your mind control over the eggs.

After your demonstrations with pepper and eggs and water, kids may want to add both these "tricks" to their repertoires of magic. When performing the egg maneuver, they should prepare the glasses ahead of time so that the audience does not know about the dissolved salt. The magician can put a tiny piece of tape on the bottom of the salt-water glass so that he won't confuse the two.

Jumping Dime

Dimes can "jump" (and so can the roofs of houses during hurricanes) when they are sucked into a swiftly moving air stream. To demonstrate, you will need only a dime and a saucer.

Place a dime on a table about ½″ from the edge. Put a saucer on the table a few inches beyond the dime. Lean over so that your face is about 5″ away from the dime, and blow a sudden

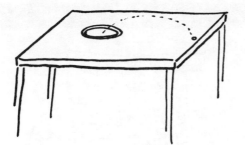

strong blast of air across the top of the coin. It will obediently jump into the dish. (You will probably have to practice this a few times to gauge the distance of the dime from the saucer and the distance of your face from the dime when blowing.)

The jumping dime performs according to a simple rule of air pressure. The faster a stream of air moves, the less it presses on anything along-side it. Things like dimes—and roofs of houses —seem to be sucked into a stream of moving air because normal air pressure on the side is stronger and pushes the objects into the moving stream. This is exactly what happens when you blow across the top of the dime.

Mysterious Lifts

Every time your child sips a drink through a straw, he is taking advantage of air pressure to lift the liquid. When a child sucks on a straw, he is forcing the air already in the drinking glass to push the liquid into the straw.

For a dramatic demonstration of how air pressure can lift liquids very high, you will need:

    3 or 4 clear plastic straws
    tape
    grape juice (or colored water)
    clear drinking glass

Tape the straws together to make a very "tall" straw. Pour grape juice in the drinking glass and set it on the floor. Then let your child suck up the juice through the long straw. He can easily see the liquid moving up through the straw as air pressure pushes the level of the liquid in the glass down.

FOR A "MAGIC" PAPER LIFT, YOU WILL NEED:
    large paper cup
    scissors

piece of heavyweight paper—construction paper or an envelope

Cut a hole in the bottom of the paper cup with the scissors. Then put the cup on the piece of paper with the bottom up. When a child sucks through the hole and lifts the cup, the paper will stay attached to the cup.

Even a very young child can get a kick out of doing this "trick" for his friends. Air, of course, holds the paper up. When a child sucks air from the cup, he is creating a vacuum—making less air in the cup and more air outside the cup. The air outside the cup presses under the paper and holds it up.

Electric Balloons

On a cool day when the kids are already wearing sweaters, try this balloon game that demonstrates the presence of static electricity in the air. Make sure that you have at least 3 or 4 balloons for each child.

Have the kids blow up a bunch of balloons and tie them at the ends. Then show them how to rub the balloons on their sweaters until they stick. Kids will get a kick of walking around covered with balloons.

Rubbing the balloons on the wool sweaters produces static electricity, the same kind that we feel when we run across a wool rug and touch something made of metal. Scientists have learned about electricity, you can explain, by rubbing different things together. In subsequent experiments, they have learned to make electricity run through wires in order to make other things move.

MEASURES

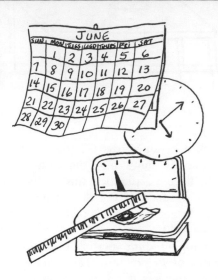

Measures are not easy for children to grasp as abstractions. Therefore, I think it best to personalize them whenever possible—through cooking together, weekly weigh-ins, associating regular times of day with hours on a clock face. Like all branches of science, measures are a way of understanding and bringing order to the world around us. The following activities aim to show that measures are routine tools for convenience in daily living.

"Me" Measures

A birthday, New Year's Day, the beginning of the school year, before going to the doctor for an annual medical checkup—these are all natural occasions for a child to realize it makes sense to measure himself. With Americans becoming increasingly health conscious, even a very young child will want to make a habit of self-checks on his growth.

When he goes to the doctor for a physical for example, at the very minimum the doctor's notes will include: the day of the visit, the time of the visit, the height, weight, and body temperature of the child. You can do this at home and kill two birds with one stone—make doctor visits less traumatic and acquaint your child with the measuring devices used for these simplest of notations:

    date (a calendar)
    time (clock)
    height (ruler or yardstick)
    weight (scale)
    body temperature (thermometer)

If you and your family are really into personal health, you might want to keep your notes from self-checkups in a special diary. If not, at least write down for your child what he discovers about himself so that he has a record.

With the calendar (we will make one in Chapter Ten), let him find the month and day of his checkup. Add the year, of course.

With the clock, let him note the time of his checkup . . . noting morning—A.M.—or afternoon—P.M.

With the ruler, you can measure his height. Write it down both in inches (39 inches, for example) and feet and inches (3 feet, 3 inches). For fun, let him use the ruler to measure the length in inches of his hand and his foot. Most people are surprised to learn that everyone's foot is the same size as their forearm (measure from inside elbow to inside wrist). If you have a flexible measure, a child can have a field day measuring every part of himself—his toes, fingers, even ears.

With the scale, record his weight. Remind him of how much he weighed when he was born and of how much he has grown.

Finally, with the thermometer take his temperature. Show him how the thermometer is marked with a red line at 98.6° F to indicate normal body temperature. A higher temperature than that, of course, is one indication of an infection—a reason you need to take his temperature when you think he is sick.

If you do keep a regular home record of everybody's self-checks, you might want to include a photograph, too. When a child looks back over the record to check his growth, he can both read and see how he has changed.

Lemonade

Making lemonade, orange juice, or Kool-Aid is a good time to introduce kids to liquid measurements of cups, quarts, even gallons . . . if you should be making a large quantity.

HAVE ON HAND:

1 can of frozen lemonade or juice (any size)
pitcher for mixing
8 oz. measuring cup
empty quart bottle or 32 oz. measuring cup

Mix up the lemonade with water in the pitcher according to the directions on the can. Then have your child pour lemonade from the pitcher into the 8 oz. measuring cup, filling it to the top. Next, have him pour the 8 oz. of lemonade into the quart bottle or 32 oz. measuring cup. Have him repeat the process until the quart container is full—and ask him, how many cups did it take to fill the quart?

He can then measure the rest of the lemonade and figure out how many cups of lemonade come from a can of frozen juice (depending on whatever size you are using). You can, of course, introduce liquid measures with water at the kitchen sink, but it's more fun to drink the lemonade you have learned to measure.

Sugar Bowl

Next time you are filling your sugar cannister or sugar bowl, let your child help and he can learn something about dry measures with cups and spoons. For simplicity, start with a sugar bowl and a set of measuring spoons.

YOU WILL NEED:

1 cup of sugar
1 set of graduated measuring spoons
1 sugar bowl

Pour the sugar into the cup and give your child the spoons. Show him the big tablespoon and let him use it to spoon the sugar into the bowl. To make the measures accurate, show him how to tap the tablespoon against the side of the cup so that the sugar in the spoon is level. When he has finished, ask him how many spoonfuls it took to fill the bowl.

This sounds painfully easy and is—but the practice in measuring the sugar accurately will come in handy when you are cooking together.

Metric System

If your kids are in school, they may already have been introduced to the metric system. Since it is becoming more common throughout the world, and will someday be a standard of measure in the U.S., you might want to invest in your own meter stick—measured off in decimeters and centimeters—to have in the hall closet.

Have a little fun with the meter stick by making a body picture (see Chapter One) and then letting your child use the meter stick to measure himself in the metric system. Just as he did with the ruler, he can measure parts of his body in decimeters and centimeters and write them right on the body picture.

A meter, by the way, is slightly more than a yard. If the metric system is unfamiliar to you, you might want to measure yourself in meters as well.

CHAPTER TEN

Unbirthdays and Other Red-letter Days

Preview:

A FAMILY CALENDAR

MOBILES FOR ALL SEASONS

COSTUMES FOR ANY OCCASION

MAD HATTERS

BIRTHDAYS COME ONCE A YEAR

UNBIRTHDAYS COME ANY TIME

CHRISTMAS AND THE FOURTH OF JULY, HALlowe'en, and Thanksgiving—rare is the family with small children that can ignore these colorful holidays, especially when costumes and/or presents are part of the traditional celebration. In any public library you can find dozens of books specializing in holiday lore, and at the end of this chapter, I include a few of my favorite holiday ideas.

But any time you are feeling festive can be the inspiration for a special family occasion, and sometimes even the beginning of a new family custom. One family I know has had a great deal of fun over the years hosting an annual August "watermelon luau" for their neighbors. Another family found an excuse to have more birthday dinners at home by observing the birthdays of family favorites—from Mickey Mouse to Beethoven. With imagination, you can make even the most ordinary day a date to circle on your calendar.

A FAMILY CALENDAR

Like most frazzled parents, I keep a desk calendar that is crammed with the details of everyone's life, from my business appointments to the kids' doctor checkups to my mother-in-law's birthday. But why should only one person try to keep track of everything? A few years ago I decided to share the burden by hanging up in the kitchen a BIG wall calendar, the largest I could find with enough space around each date so that everyone had room to write in important memos.

The kids wrote in their birthdays first, of course, but I also discovered that having their weekly activities listed alongside ours improved our communication as a family. When they could see just how busy a day was ahead, they became less likely to make impossible requests. Now, we try to plan together each week, particularly the after-school hours on school days when there is invariably a conflict. In short, because we can all clearly see the (literal) handwriting on the wall, we have become not only a better-organized family, but also a more relaxed and tolerant one.

If you can't find a calendar big enough to suit your needs, you can easily make one. Let the kids help you; this could be a once-monthly afternoon project. You will need:

1 large sheet brown wrapping paper (3′ × 3′ is a good size; children tend to have big handwriting)
small desk calendar for guide to dates
Magic Markers
ruler or yardstick

Preschoolers can watch while you draw the calendar page; older kids, of course, can do the work under your supervision. First, mark the sheet off into days and weeks, using the small calendar as a guide. Use the yardstick to make straight lines with the Magic Markers. Write the month at the top of the page and then fill in the boxes with the days of the week and the dates. Then let the kids write in upcoming events from their schedules.

If your boxes are large enough, they can draw in pictures, too, or paste in photos, newspaper clippings, or other reminders. Some children like to embellish such a calendar with seasonal sketches around the edges—snow scenes for January, for example. A good month in which to start a family calendar and to keep your child's interest would be the month of his birthday. Once he has marked off his day, he will begin to feel the sense of anticipation that makes keeping a calendar work.

MOBILES FOR ALL SEASONS

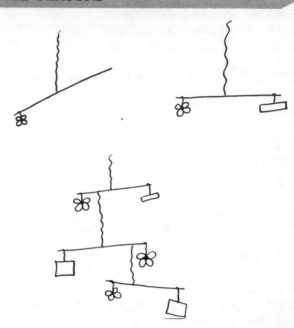

To capture the spirit of any time of year, construct a mobile with your child that is keyed to the passing season. Hang snowflakes for winter, flowers for spring, vegetables for summer, leaves for fall.

The directions below are for a mobile made with yarn, straws, and lightweight paper objects, the easiest materials to guarantee balance. Just one of these "hanging sculptures" festooning a window adds a touch of gaiety. Several increase the effect.

If your child enjoys making mobiles, you can help him to create custom-made versions to mark any special occasion: flags for the Fourth of July; photographs of everyone in the family for a present to a grandparent; pictures cut from magazines of things a friend likes for a personalized birthday gift. For his own room, a child can invent countless "Me" mobiles.

MATERIALS:

    brightly colored yarn (or heavy string or thread) cut in 2′ lengths

    a "hanging" string—a longer length of yarn, probably close to 3′

    package of plastic straws

    paper shapes—cut from construction paper (use jar lids to trace circles; box tops for rectangles and squares)

    glue stick

    pencil with sharp point

For an uncomplicated trial run, show your child how a mobile works on the principle of balance.

First, tie a hanging string in the center of a straw. Then, cut out of the construction paper 2 shapes (use the jar lid and the box top to trace a circle and a square). Use the pencil to poke a hole near the top of one of the shapes. Now thread one end of the shorter pieces of yarn through the hole. Tie the other end of the yarn securely to one end of the straw. Hold up the hanging string so that your child can see the straw is unbalanced.

Next, thread the other shape and attach it to the other end of the straw. When you hold up the hanging string this time, your child can see that objects of equal weight are needed on each end of the straw to make the mobile balance. Once he grasps the idea, you can show him how to tie on other lengths of yarn to other straws to construct a more elaborate mobile.

COSTUMES FOR ANY OCCASION

Most children look forward to contriving a disguise for Hallowe'en, but why not encourage them to dream up costumes to make other occasions more fun. Suggest they come to the Thanksgiving dinner table as Indians and Pilgrims, for example. Or, at a family birthday party, suggest that everyone, grown-ups included, wear a funny hat. If you absolutely find it too undignified to don a costume yourself, then let the kids satisfy their dress-up cravings at neighborhood "unbirthday" parties.

You don't need an attic with a trunkful of grandmother's fabulous old clothes to create clever costumes. In fact, I've found that simple materials work better; first, because children can do much of the designing themselves; and second, because the results are quicker, inexpensive, and disposable. From grocery boxes, paper bags, plastic garbage bags, old sheets, and worn men's shirts, you can design a closetful of memorable getups.

Of Bags and Boxes

Grocery Boxes

All you need to get the kids started on costumes are boxes large enough to cover their bodies. A grown-up must prepare the box by cutting holes for arms and head (or, if the head is going to be inside, holes for seeing and breathing). For starters, try the following:

MAILBOX: For this costume, don't cut a hole for the head. Instead, cut a mail slot so the child can look out. Cut the arm holes so that the box is comfortable to wear.

Now get out your poster paints. Paint the top third of the box red, the bottom two-thirds blue. Finish off the mailbox by using white paint to letter U. S. Mail on the front.

SCHOOL BUS: Cut the arm and head holes so the child can wear the box horizontally rather than vertically. Cover the box with glued-on yellow construction paper. Then use Magic Markers for the decorations: black for windows and headlights and to letter the name of the school district on the side of the bus. Use colored Magic Markers to draw children's faces in the windows of the bus. Complete the costume by finding a driver's cap for your child to wear.

ROBOT OR SPACEMAN: Cover the box with aluminum foil. Draw or glue on buttons, knobs, etc. Complete the costume with a full-head mask (Chapter Four).

HAUNTED HOUSE: After you have cut the head and arm holes, cut windows and doors. Don't cut out the cardboard completely; leave flaps that look like swinging shutters and creaky doors. Use poster or spray paint (black or dark green) to make the house look old and musty. Then cut long sprigs of trailing ivy from your own house or garden and Scotch tape them all over the house. A child can wear any kind of scary mask to complete the costume.

Once your child starts thinking about how to

adapt the box shape, he'll come up with other ideas: a dice cube, a gift package, a cereal box, a doghouse, a skyscraper, even a chest of drawers. To personify his favorite comic strip character, he might buy or make a face mask that looks like the character. Then he can use the box to complete his costume by covering it with glued-on comic strips in which the character appears.

Paper Bags

Paper bags are wonderfully versatile for making all kinds of masks and costumes. You may already have tried the "buckskins" in Chapter Four. For a simpler all-in-one garment, use one large grocery bag for each child that will serve as both mask and costume.

As with boxes, a grown-up must first cut out holes for arms, large holes for eyes. Then, let the children use crayons or Magic Markers to draw giant faces on the front of the grocery bags. Favorites with preschoolers: pirate, clown, queen, king, witch, TV character, dog, cat (in fact, almost any animal, although he may have to tell you what it is supposed to be!), magician, soldier, and so on.

If a mask will suffice to disguise the wearer, use smaller grocery bags that cover only the head. Again, cut big holes for eyes and mouth. From extra bags cut out ears for rabbits and dogs; trunks for elephants. Use Magic Markers to color spots for leopards and stripes for zebras.

Strips of fringed paper attached to the back of the bag make horse manes; strips of paper curled with scissors can suggest a tousle-headed lion. Glue on feathers for birds and Indians.

Making costumes from grocery bags is a good project for those times you have to be indoors. Children enjoy the making as much as the wearing; hence, the end results need not be realistic or perfect. Paper bags are also a quick and easy way to improvise costumes for young actors who like to put on plays.

Of Sheets and Shirts

Old sheets can be recycled into costumes that are more durable than those made from paper bags and boxes. If you sew, I'm sure you can think of all kinds of ways to stitch up fancy fairy dresses, clown suits, or Indian leggings. Togas and ghost gowns, on the other hand, require only deft draping and tying.

In between those extremes, I've had good luck using old sheets to cut out simple tunics which the kids can decorate with Magic Markers any way they like, often with just their names or odd pictures. These can serve as smocks for painting or messy artwork, too.

MATERIALS:
old sheet
stapler
scissors
Magic Markers

Fold the sheet in half the wide way and lay it on a table. For a pattern, use one of your child's nightgowns or bathrobes. Or, you can lay the

sheet on the floor and have the child lie down on his back so that you can trace around him. In either case, use a Magic Marker to draw the pattern.

Cut out the pattern with scissors, cutting through both layers of the sheet. Cut a circle for the neck and head out of the folded edge.

Next, use a stapler to fasten together the open sides (or sew with a simple basting stitch by hand or on a sewing machine). Turn the tunic inside out. Now your part is done.

Give the finished garment to your child to decorate with Magic Markers. A red cross alone can indicate a doctor or nurse outfit. Fringe the bottom for an Indian squaw dress. Draw on spots or stripes to suggest an animal. Older children might enjoy making elaborate designs of many colors, such as fabric designers do. If you are using a patterned sheet rather than a solid-colored one, the pattern may lend itself to some undreamed-of reincarnation.

One way to save yourself the trouble of making sheet tunics is to make it a habit to save worn men's shirts. You will probably have to cut off long sleeves to fit a preschooler, but the shirt shape is dandy for decorating as you did with the tunics. Many nursery schools and kindergartens traditionally suggest old shirts for painting smocks.

MAD HATTERS

A simple paper topper adds a touch of pizazz to a humble party. Hats are almost expected for birthdays or New Year's Eve, but don't forget "bonnets" for Easter or parade gear for the Fourth of July. And any time you feel zany, try asking the family to come to the dinner table as "mad hatters." Crown the youngest child "King for a Day" with the paper crown described in Chapter Two. Or try one of the no-fail designs below.

Paper-plate Hat

MATERIALS:
    paper plate
    paper doily
    glue stick
    crayons or Magic Markers
    scissors
    Scotch tape
    ribbons

Let your child use the Magic Markers or crayons to color the bottom of the paper plate the color she would like her hat to be. The rim of the plate will be the brim; the inside will be the crown.

For decoration, glue bits of a paper doily around the underside of the brim and on the top of the crown. Then cut a slit on each side of the plate near the crown. Slide the ribbon through the slits and under the plate and tie under the chin.

Puritan Cap

For Thanksgiving, suggest that the girls wear a Puritan cap, the boys an Indian chief headdress.

MATERIALS:
    paper bag
    white paper doily
    string or ribbon
    glue stick
    scissors

Again, make sure that the paper bag is an appropriate size for your child's head. First, cut the front panel out of the bag. Next cut off the sides and back panels so that you have something that looks like a cap.

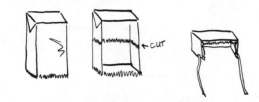

Cut the doily in strips and glue the "lace" around the side edges of the bag and across the top so that the trimming frames the face. Then cut a very small hole in each side of the bag. Through each hole pull a ribbon or string, being sure to make a large knot at the bag end for security. Tie under the chin.

Indian Chief Headdress

MATERIALS:
    large paper bag
    Scotch tape and/or stapler
    crayons or Magic Markers
    scissors

Starting at the open end, cut up one side of the bag. Then cut out the heavy bottom. Flatten out the bag (now a rectangle of heavy paper) on a table. For a sturdy headband, fold under one of the long sides of the paper to a depth of about 3". Scotch tape the underside of the band to the paper.

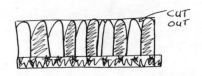

On the top side of the paper, first use the crayons and Magic Markers to draw a headband design. A solid color will do, but you might want to embellish the band with geometric figures or birds and animals. Next, draw the feathers. Then color the feathers different colors. Cut out the feathers, try on the headdress to adjust the headband for size, and tape or staple the ends of the band together.

Newspaper Hats

Soldier Hat

MATERIALS:
   1 sheet newspaper, approximately 23″ × 30″
   strips of colored tissue paper or comics, about 12″ × 6″
   Scotch tape or stapler

Fold the newspaper in half and then in half again. Next fold the folded corners toward the center. Then fold up the bottom twice on each side of the hat. Try on the hat for size. Scotch tape or staple the ends on each side of the opening so that the hat fits.

Decorate the hat with a pompon made from the colored strips of paper (red, white, and blue for Fourth of July; multicolors for New Year's; black and orange for Hallowe'en; and so forth). Stack the strips of colored paper together and on the long side, cut a fringe about 3″ deep. Starting at the short side, roll up the uncut edges as tightly as you can. Secure the rolled portion with Scotch tape. Attach the finished pompon to the top of the hat with more Scotch tape or with a stapler.

(If your child wishes to make similar hats for his dolls or stuffed animals, you will find in Chapter Two directions for a hat made with a standard-sized 8½″ × 11″ sheet of office paper.)

Witch Hat

MATERIALS:
   2 double sheets of newspaper
   Scotch tape
   crayons or Magic Markers
   construction paper (optional)
   scissors (optional)
   glue stick (optional)

Place one double sheet of newspaper on top of the other so that you are working with a 4-layer thickness. Starting at one of the corners, roll the paper into a cone shape. Tape the rolled paper lightly so that the cone will hold its shape while your child tries on the hat for size. After adjusting for fit, tape securely along the edge of the paper that makes the cone. To make a brim for the front of the hat, fold back the wide end of the cone. Let your child draw moons, stars, and

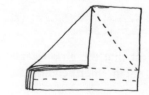

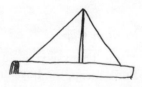

other witch symbols on the hat with Magic Markers, or he can glue on decorations cut from construction paper.

If your child insists on having a black witch hat, you can make a similar cone out of black construction paper. You may have to cut off the brim, however, as construction paper is not as pliable as newspaper. Perhaps the impromptu advantages of using readily available newspaper will forestall any complaints. Or, you can tell him about Merlin and King Arthur and call this hat a sorcerer's cap from the outset, so that witches never enter the picture at all.

Oatmeal Box Hats

A large oatmeal box can easily be transformed into a top hat with construction paper and glue. Depending on the mood of the moment, your child can choose appropriate colors of paper to tip his hat as Abe Lincoln, a magician, a leprechaun, an English bobby, Uncle Sam, and probably several other characters you or I haven't thought of yet. Follow the basic directions below.

Abe Lincoln Stovepipe Hat or Magician Top Hat

MATERIALS:
1 large oatmeal box
black construction paper
Scotch tape
glue stick
scissors
shirt cardboard (or lightweight cardboard)

First, cut construction paper so that it will cover the outside of the box. Then glue the paper firmly on the "crown."

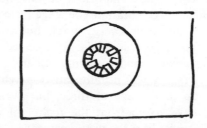

To make a brim, use the circular opening of the box for a pattern. Trace the circle on a piece of construction paper. Inside the circle draw tabs that you will use to glue the brim to the inside of the hat. Outside the circle draw a larger circle (allow 3″ for an Abe Lincoln stovepipe; a smaller brim for a magician top hat).

To give the brim extra strength, glue the construction paper onto a lightweight piece of cardboard, such as a shirt cardboard. Now cut out the larger circle first. Then cut out the smaller circle, leaving the tabs intact. The tabs can be glued to either the inside or outside of the crown, but I think they work best on the outside. Cover them by cutting another strip of black construction paper about 1″ wide and gluing it in place at the base of the crown. With a bit of decoration, this topper can become an Uncle Sam stovepipe, a leprechaun's lid, a drum major's shako, or anything else your child fancies. Hats off!

BIRTHDAYS COME ONCE A YEAR

No doubt about it, a child looks forward to his birthday as *the* most important day of the year. How much of a celebration you stage depends on your time and your energy level, but tradition decrees only three essentials: a cake with candles, ice cream, and presents. Sharing these within the family will usually satisfy parents and children up to the age of three, but eventually you will have to confront the reality of a preschooler's social life: the birthday party.

Why some parents of very young children feel the need to plan an extravaganza baffles me. Imported entertainment (ponies, clowns, magicians, even chefs to show the kids how to bake cookies) or expensive outings (movies or restaurants) are admittedly fun, but far from necessary. One four-year-old I know presided over a caterpillar ride which his mother had had an amusement park erect in his back yard to amuse the guests. When things get to that extreme, I suspect the parents are competing with each other in a "can-you-top-this" contest rather than focusing on the enjoyment of the children.

My philosophy about birthday parties boils down to this: KEEP IT SIMPLE. Spend imagination, not money. Both you and the kids will have a more relaxed time, and will look forward to next year, rather than dreading the need for an elaborate encore.

Ground-rule Guidelines

Perhaps the following guidelines, which have worked for me and for other parents, will help you to streamline the next birthday at your house.

1. Many busy families plan two birthday parties for each child. One is a private family celebration, maybe a special dinner at home or an outing, and is always observed on the actual date of the child's birthday. The other party is for the child's friends, held on the birthday itself or on a weekend, whichever time is more convenient for you. This two-party custom satisfies the child's need to feel important on his day, and takes the pressure off you to entertain on a day that may conflict with your schedule.

2. Parties for children under four are risky, if not an invitation to disaster. If you must have one, be sure the party is short and loaded with action. Plot an hour of activities divided into ten-minute segments. Providing something new every ten minutes will help to keep the children's attention and avoid homesickness.

By the time they are four, most kids have had a taste of nursery school and socializing and will be better guests. They can speak clearly and can follow simple directions. While most still take an afternoon nap, they can give this up occasionally or sleep less and survive without being cranky. Also, you can usually trust that four-year-olds are toilet trained.

3. A good old standby rule for the number of guests: invite no more than the age of the birthday child. That is, fours may invite four friends, fives may invite five, and so on.

4. For children six and under, allow one hour maximum for the length of the party. Never forget that small children have a short attention span. For any age, allow two hours at the outside limit. One and a half hours should be plenty. Better to have a short party where no one goes home bored and/or irritable than to have the festivities disintegrate into an unruly group of youngsters.

5. Write or phone the invitation to the guests' parents, specifying the time the party will begin and end.

6. When children arrive at the party, make sure the parents know what time the party will be over. Double-check to find out who will call for the child so that you won't have to cope with leftover kids after the other guests have gone. Or, tell the parents ahead of time that you will take the children home yourself. It's worth the extra time and trouble to make sure the party ends on time—and on an upbeat note.

An Easy Routine

1. *Begin with play.* Children who come to a party are bound to be excited. I find it's a good idea to begin the party right on time with outdoor play, if possible, or an indoor game. Late-comers can join in as they arrive. But some kind of physical activity help kids to let off steam and feel relaxed.

2. *Open presents.* Don't overdo the suspense. Let the birthday boy or girl tear open the packages so that the other children can have a look, too.

3. *Eat.* Let the kids settle down a bit, with whatever menu you have planned or with simple birthday cake and ice cream. Sitting down at a table is practical, if only to control the mess.

4. *Have favors at the table for the guests.* No child who brings a present to a birthday party wants to go home empty-handed. Try to have something at his place—a party hat, an inexpensive toy—anything he can proudly display on his return home.

5. *End with games—and prizes.* Now is the time for something more organized—if you are that ambitious, the children are old enough, and there is time. For easy games, try Milk-carton Bowling (Chapter Four), Beanbag Basketball (Chapter One), or Go Fishing (later on in this chapter).

If you're feeling artsy-craftsy, you can help the kids to make their own party hats, masks, or costumes (as suggested earlier in this chapter). Or look through other chapters in this book for a simple toy they could make to take home (directions for clothespin dolls or soldiers and a spool railway engine are both in Chapter Five). For any craft activity, save time and confusion by giving each child a paper bag containing the needed materials. Tie a ribbon around each bag and write on individual names.

When the guests make something, you needn't award prizes—in fact, prizes may discourage the less creative who worry they haven't a chance to win anything. But if the game is competitive (bowling, for example), a tiny reward doesn't hurt. It just gives the child something else to take home. As long as everyone has a favor to take home anyway, most preschoolers won't begrudge the lucky one who earns something extra.

Games are part of a standard birthday party routine, but you don't really have to do anything after the cake if you're not so inclined. If you have a big back yard, the kids may be ready for more outdoor free play. Older children probably prefer tossing a Frisbee, passing a football, or playing tag.

Birthday Bonuses

To make the party table festive, you and your child can make a Birthday Tree for a centerpiece. Design Button-people Place Cards for each guest. At the conclusion of the feast, bring out a piñata to surprise everyone with bits of candy.

Birthday Tree

Follow the directions in Chapter Six for mounting a branch to make an "Indoor Tree." For a seasonal birthday tree, glue or hang on the branch objects appropriate to the month: white cotton balls for January, for example, red-felt hearts for February, or orange-paper pumpkin faces for October.

For gaiety any time of year, just tie bow ribbons of many colors on the tree, or attach blown-up balloons.

To make the tree more personal, suggest to your child that he draw or cut out pictures from magazines of things he likes or likes to do. Mount the cutouts on construction paper with glue and tie them on the branch for a "Me Tree."

The possibilities for festooning a birthday tree are endless. One child I know decorated his with tiny toys—trinkets from Cracker Jack boxes and small plastic soldiers and trucks—attached with loops of yarn much as one would hang orna-ments on a Christmas tree. After the birthday was over, the tree went on permanent display in his room.

Button-people Place Cards

Place cards at a birthday party are nice for preschoolers if only because they make the children feel like special guests. You can make simple ones by folding an envelope in half and then writing each child's name on one side—4″ × 6″ index cards fold well, too.

If you are feeling more energetic, look through your button box for extra 2-holed buttons. The button glued to a folded envelope, index card, or piece of construction paper becomes a face which you and your child can embellish.

MATERIALS:
   2-holed button (at least 1″ in diameter)
   envelope, index card 4″ × 6″, or construction paper
   airplane cement
   crayons or Magic Markers
   trimmings: bits of colored construction paper, newspaper, cloth, yarn, glitter, etc.

First, fold in half the paper or envelope that you will use for the card. You will work on only one side of the fold.

Next, glue the button "face" onto the left side of the place card near the edge. Let your child use crayons or Magic Markers to draw around the button, adding hair, hats, ears, and so forth. Show him how just a hat can make the button look like a cowboy, an Indian, or a clown. Then in the blank space at the right of the card, write in the name of the guest.

For a more detailed place card, glue the button on the card so that there is room for your child to draw arms and legs and "clothes" underneath the "face." Or, if he likes, he can cut out limbs (or skirts, pants, shoes, or hats) from newspaper and cloth and glue them onto the card underneath the button. For "hair," run a line of glue around the button, then press on bits of yarn or cotton. To make the button "smile," use a red Magic Marker to draw a mouth on the "face" beneath the hole "eyes."

Piñata

Children in Mexico always anticipate piñatas at Christmastime, but best of all is a birthday piñata because it honors one child alone. This project takes time and trouble. You will have to do most of the work, but little kids find piñatas fascinating.

MATERIALS:
1 round balloon, inflated
paintbrush
newspaper—cut into 1″ strips
colored tissue paper—cut into 1″ strips
paste made from flour and water in a bowl
small pieces of wrapped hard candy

First, inflate the balloon and tie it securely. Then, with the paintbrush, apply flour and water paste to the balloon. One by one, wrap the strips of newspaper over the paste around the inflated balloon. Be sure the balloon is completely covered with the paper. If necessary, dip some of the newspaper strips into the paste to make them stick. Allow the balloon to dry for 2 days.

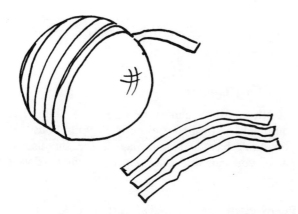

Next, apply more paste to the hardened balloon and apply the strips of tissue paper (one color or many), just as you did the newspaper. Again, allow the balloon to dry for another 2 days.

The final steps are easy for even little ones to do. Show your child how to use a straight pin to pop the balloon inside the hardened shell. Then, cut a hole in the top with a sharp knife. Let your child put the candy inside the piñata as a surprise for his guests. Children in Mexico break the piñata with a stick. You may prefer to let the children reach inside for their treats.

To decorate the piñata, glue on bits of construction paper before putting the candy inside. A balloon covered with orange tissue paper can become a jack-o'-lantern with black eyes, nose, and snaggle-toothed mouth. Add green around the hole to look like the base of the stem. White tissue paper makes a good background for a clown face. Add round red cheeks and nose and a green or purple mouth; cut out sad or happy eyes to give the face expression.

Oriental Lanterns

String up a dozen of these charming "lanterns" over the birthday table or in the back yard for a colorful effect.

MATERIALS:
construction paper—several sheets in different colors (larger sizes make more distinctive lanterns)
glue stick
crayons or Magic Markers
scissors

Cut a piece of construction paper so that it is ½″ longer than it is wide. Fold the paper in half the long way.

Hold the paper with the folded edge at the bottom and the open edges at the top. On the folded edge cut slits at regular intervals to within ½″ of the top.

Open the paper. Overlap the two side edges and glue them together. From another piece of construction paper cut a handle and glue it across the top of the lantern.

Surprise Birthday "Cake"

If one birthday cake delights a child, two are even better. This fake one, made of boxes filled with small presents, will please children of all ages. Serve it at a family birthday dinner just before the real cake arrives. Or help your child make one for a special friend. The time it takes justifies the surprise.

MATERIALS:
   2 boxes, one slightly larger than the other (big enough to hold the smaller box). A deep box will look more like a "cake" than a shallow one
   tiny presents, wrapped individually (a toy soldier, a toy truck, a whistle, etc.)
   wrapping paper and ribbon
   cake frosting
   birthday candles and holders

Put the tiny presents inside the smaller box and wrap the smaller box as if it were a single gift. Set aside.

Now decorate the lid of the larger box with frosting to look like a birthday cake. Place the smaller box in the bottom of the larger box. Put on the decorated lid, add candles and light, and the surprise is ready to serve.

The Feast: Birthday Party Food

My best advice about birthday party menus is to repeat in a loud voice: KEEP IT SIMPLE. Imag-

ination, not money, is the key. Many a plate of chicken à la king has gone untouched by an unimpressed preschooler. Birthday cake and ice cream (add juice or milk if you have to) is more than sufficient. Don't be surprised if some little kids do not eat a morsel at birthday parties. The excitement of being there and seeing the cake is enough.

If you feel compelled to offer more food, however, hot dogs and potato chips are almost always foolproof and popular. For novelty, you might try:

1. "Breakfast Sundae" (Chapter One): I mention this favorite of mine at the risk of violating tradition, but some mothers I know have had good luck serving a rainbow of yogurt flavors instead of ice cream.

2. Open-"face" Sandwiches (Chapter Three): This simple variation on the old peanut butter and raisins standby will cause at least one guest to chuckle.

3. "Veggie" sticks for nibbles instead of candy. Put them on the birthday table in paper boats (Chapter Two).

4. "Rainbow Eggs" (Chapter Five): But remember that some young children do have egg allergies. Be sure to check ahead.

5. "Cheese Fondue" (Chapter Three): a "meal in a pot" that requires adult supervision, but is new and palatable to most kids. If they don't like the cheese mixture, they can munch on the pieces of bread.

Two Easy Games

Both of these games require little skill. The equipment is probably already in your house. If you don't have a small magnet for the fishing game, you can find one at your local hardware store.

Penny Pitch

MATERIALS:
   5 pennies for each player
   empty oatmeal box or coffee can

Each child takes turns trying to pitch his 5 pennies into the box or can. The player with the best aim wins. To make the game more challenging in each successive round, move the can a foot or so farther from the pitching line. Although the high scorer may win a prize, let each player keep his 5 pennies to take home.

Go Fishing

MATERIALS:
magnet
ruler
Scotch tape
string—1 piece about 18″ long
construction paper in different colors
paper clips
scissors
crayons or Magic Markers

Everyone playing the game will use the same rod to go fishing. To make the rod, tie one end of the piece of string onto one end of the ruler. Wrap Scotch tape around the string to make sure it doesn't slip off the ruler. Tie the other end of the string around the middle of the magnet.

Draw fish on different colors of construction paper. Cut out the fish and write the name of each player or a number on each one. Fasten a paper clip on the mouth of each fish.

Use a small rug for a "pond." Put the fish in the pond, and let each child take a turn with the fishing rod trying to catch his own name.

UNBIRTHDAYS COME ANY TIME

There's no reason why a child should have to wait for his birthday to have a party. An "unbirthday" is a fine excuse, especially if a child's real birthday comes during the summer and he misses the chance to host his school friends. Some other good causes to celebrate might be:

A Half Birthday

Every six months of age counts a lot to little kids, especially those under twelve. If you ask anyone over six how old he is, he's likely to add on the fraction of a year that makes him that much older. A seven-year-old likes to tell you he's really "seven and a half" or even "seven and three quarters." Why not legitimatize that half birthday with a simple party? Carry out the theme by serving half a birthday cake, half portions of ice cream, and cups of milk half full. It may sound zany, but kids love it.

Brown-bag Toy Swap

A practical way to recycle toys a child has tired of is to suggest that he swap them with friends. You can add an element of surprise to this type of party by asking each guest to bring an old toy (or toys) wrapped in a brown lunch bag with a ribbon. When the time comes to "open the presents," arrange them on a table or in a box. Ask each child to cover his eyes or wear a handkerchief blindfold as he makes his pick.

Some parents I know have found this kind of swap is a good way to dispose of playthings that pile up in an attic or garage, often in good condition, but simply not used. It's also a popular activity for children in a neighborhood play group, and, in an indirect way, encourages sharing.

Pet Party

Every pet-owning family has to live through at least one pet birthday party. Dogs and cats are the likely lucky honorees, but some youngsters like to observe the birthdays of gerbils, goldfish, canaries—everything that lives and breathes. For safety at such parties, it's important to limit the number of animal guests, since dogs, in particular, are apt to take a dislike to one another. Every animal should be on a leash or in a cage.

To keep pet parties simple, provide cupcakes

and/or popsicles for the humans, and appropriate pet food for the animals. Small animals might get their treats in paper cups; dogs, however, are usually happy with large dog biscuits.

One last word: Pet parties should ALWAYS be held outdoors and with an adult present.

Talking Back to Television

YOU CAN READ DOZENS OF BOOKS WITH TIPS ON parenting, including mine, but one nagging question still perplexes most households of the eighties: How do families cope with television?

It's a problem of paramount concern to me because of my dual role as a producer of kids' shows and as a parent of two young children. Those of us in the television industry obviously want large audiences for our programs and constantly research ways to attract them. But any parent knows that children are not very discriminating viewers. They may prefer one program to another, yet given the option of watching TV or not watching TV, they are apt to watch anything. The very phrase "children's television" is misleading. Kids don't watch only "kiddie" shows; "children's television" means whatever children watch, whether it's aimed at them or not.

When you consider that preschoolers are at home more than any other group of children, you realize they are inevitably exposed to the possibility of watching more television than any other age group. The actual number of hours they spend in front of the set may surprise you. Current research indicates that the average preschooler watches thirty-three hours of TV a week, almost five hours (4.7, to be exact) a day.

To weight the impact of that hefty chunk of time, remember that, by definition, preschoolers are young children who must be in the care of an adult at all times. They cannot decide on their own to go to a movie or a baseball game; most of them are not even permitted to play outside of their yards alone. But turning on the TV set is something they can do by themselves, and often do when a busy adult all too easily relies on the "electronic baby-sitter" for a few moments (or several hours!) of peace. Left to themselves, preschoolers are more at the mercy of television than any other group of kids.

Some parents don't worry about TV. And I must confess that I made a tremendous mistake with Jenny, my older child, by allowing her to watch cartoons every morning, just because it was convenient. I really have no innate objection to a certain amount of cartoon watching, but it soon became obvious to me that Jenny and many of her friends used television as a total mind "turn-off." They sat passively in front of almost any program, just for something to pass the time.

Recent studies of both children and adults at the Yale School of Communications indicate that viewers' brain waves definitely change while watching television. Whether a show is "violent" or "non-violent" is incidental; in both cases the brain waves slow down. In layman's terms, that means to me that while we are watching television our brains enter a kind of half-life, a veritable "non-think." Other experts have pointed out that time spent watching television may not appear to be harmful in itself, but it is time taken away from the practice kids need to develop interpersonal skills: arguing, sharing, even simple conversation.

Now that's the bad news. Obviously, the answer to too much TV for kids is a firm parental "No." But before you padlock your set, consider whether banning television entirely from your child's life is a realistic move.

Like it or not, television has become too pervasive an influence in our daily culture to ignore. Admittedly, some of what we see on the air is a waste of time. Yet at its best, TV exposes us to news and travel programs that prompt interest in parts of the world we might not otherwise know about and provides entertainment shows whose characters become topics of common conversation. If you cut off all TV for your child, he may feel like a neighborhood pariah, someone who just doesn't know what's going on in a significant part of today's kids' world. And all of us have met the child whose parents forbid him to eat candy, but the minute his keepers are out of sight, the wholesome youngster stuffs himself with as many goodies as he can get his hands on.

Weighing the pros and cons, I think television in moderation is the pragmatic answer we have to live with. And only trial and error, not the opinions of pundits, can tell you what "moderation" means in the structure of your family life.

To find out how much television is too much television for your kids, I suggest you do a little homework. Calculate how much your own children watch TV by taking notes on their viewing habits for a week. Add up the number of hours in front of the set and ask yourself, what else could my kids be doing with that time? Thirty-three hours (if they hit the average) may fit right in with your routine and you can stop fretting.

On the other hand, thirty-three hours may be eating up time that could be spent on activities you deem more valuable. If you regard television as you do any other time-consuming activity in an overcrowded week, your priorities may become clearer.

As you contemplate what role television plays at your house, just keep in mind that most of the experts are concerned with the *amount* of TV watched rather than with the actual program *content*. A few hours of well-chosen shows can be inspiring and enriching; dozens of hours sitting alone in front of the set invite passivity. Most important, remember that your attitude toward television, like all other influences you interpret for your children, must jibe with your overall philosophy of parenting in order to succeed.

GAME PLANS FOR TV

There are lots of ways to limit TV-watching time other than with a capricious or dictatorial "No." Particularly if you're not going to be around all of the time to supervise and must either rely on a sitter or simply trust your child, you need to establish some basic guidelines. If you aim to use television to your advantage and for the advantage of your kids, then you'll be less likely to feel victimized.

One rule that has worked extremely well at our house is "no television before dark." Obviously, there can be many exceptions; I would hope you would be open-minded about an afternoon special, for example. But an issue of choice has been raised. And selectivity is fundamental to instilling in your children an attitude of critical viewing.

When the "no television before dark" rule prevails, children are forced to think of other things to do. They have more opportunities to be imaginative, to read or to make things or to exercise. Most important, they must think about how they want to use their time. Even boredom can be a kind of "creative quietude," prompting a child to expand his capacity for self-amusement.

Whatever game plan you adopt for handling television, I think you'll be more successful if you work toward some sort of relaxed compromise that permits viewing, but aims toward developing critical judgment. Some suggestions:

1. Use Television as a Reward.

It's a crude ploy, but it works. Remember that kids respond to the concrete. Make the right to watch TV a privilege by insisting that some home responsibility (chores, homework, pet care, etc.) be taken care of first. Don't let the kids' resistance weaken your resolve; you'll be making the point that the television set is something you turn *off,* as well as on.

2. Be an Active Censor.

Try to help your children understand that what they watch on television is a family concern. Let them know that you are thinking about what they choose. If you are absolutely convinced that a particular show teaches your kids the worst kind of values, make an effort to watch the program with your child at least twice. If you don't change your mind, point out during the program just what you think is dreadful. Then firmly put your foot down; no more of this show.

3. *Get Acquainted with the* Kids' Culture.

TV will never replace good books, nor should it. But try to regard television as an extra, not a substitute. Be broad-minded enough to realize that programs you don't consider to be educational or interesting can be provocative in stimulating discussions among kids. Almost every day on *Romper Room* I am amazed at how children take ideas from Superman or Spiderman or other favorite TV characters and weave them into original stories and games. Recently, I participated in a seminar of educators who were discussing youngsters' tastes in TV. I was most impressed by a young Harvard professor who had obviously watched everything his kids watched—from *Scooby-Doo and Scrappy* to *Tarzan* and *Dallas.* He knew why the children liked the shows they did, and he had had long discussions with his two little ones about the various messages these shows conveyed. His familiarity with his kids' culture helped him to communicate his opinions, his adult thinking, in their terms.

In other words, don't hesitate to disagree with *Mary Tyler Moore, Loveboat, Tom and Jerry,* or anybody else on TV. Literally speaking, your kids' language gives you one of the best forums you could possibly have for presenting your values in a positive, vivid way.

4. *Distinguish Between* Reality *and* Fantasy.

Nothing is wrong with fantasy, but kids can handle it better if they can compare the characters they meet on television with people in real life. After (or while) you are watching a show with your children, encourage them to point out the "true" things and the "pretend" things on the show. You might follow up such discussion with a visit to a police station to meet a police officer, a fire station to meet a fire fighter, a hospital to meet a paramedic, and so on. If any of your friends have occupations similar to those portrayed on TV shows, encourage your children to find out how they really live and work.

5. *Crack Down on* Commercials.

Most kids are aware that commercials interrupt a good bit of programming. Just for fun, and for your edification, too, ask them to count the number of commercials in a favorite half-hour show. See if they can tell you what the products being advertised are.

They may be able to laugh or be critical of commercials advertising products they are not at all interested in buying—soaps or beer, for example. But what about toy commercials? Here the messages can be subtle for unsophisticated and vulnerable viewers.

Watch a toy commercial with the kids. Then try to elicit from them responses to these questions:

> What does the commercial want you to like?
> How does the commercial try to make you like the product?

(Typical pitches: "It's fun!" "It's the biggest [or smallest]!" "It's exciting!" "You'll be the first on the block!" "Other kids will be jealous." And so on.)

Try to discuss with your child whether he believes what the commercial told him. Then it's easy to point out that something is not necessarily true just because someone on TV tries to make you believe his claims. Remember that consumer education begins at home. Kids need to judge ads for themselves to control their pocketbooks.

6. *Design a* Family-viewing Plan.

Take a look at the Sunday newspaper television section and go through the weekly listings with your children. This can be a very brief Sunday night routine, but from that point you can fairly intelligently predetermine what shows can and cannot be watched during the week. In other words, your child will know what is permitted beforehand and, with luck, you will be able to avoid arguments and aggravation later. Experiment with a few different game plans for TV until you find what works best for your family. Think them through, choose one, and then—make it stick.

ACTIVE TELEVISION VS. PASSIVE TELEVISION

With all of my reservations about too much TV watching for little kids, you might very well wonder why I have chosen to continue my career as a producer of children's television shows. On the set of *Romper Room* alone, I've spent eighteen years working with preschoolers.

Let me reiterate. I don't regard TV as a villain in itself. My concern is for children who just sit in front of the set like blobs, letting their brain waves go dull. I fear that when children don't interact with what they are watching, they become more and more passive. Without some kind of adult direction, kids can become so hooked on television that they are less likely to activate their own imaginations.

Those of us who produce *Romper Room* are committed to providing an alternative to passivity. Because our show aims to encourage the viewing kids to do what the kids in the studio are doing, we are totally geared toward stimulating a participatory effort at home. Maybe the children at home won't necessarily join in at the very moment the show is being aired, but we hope to start them thinking about something to do later.

Some of the gymnastics routines our kids in the studio perform, for example, we hope the kids at home will repeat later that day—and on other days, as well. Most of the "make-it" projects demonstrated on the show and collected for this book were designed with that same goal: Here's what the finished product looks like, here's a list of materials you need, and here are the directions. As often as possible, we try to limit the materials to items that are readily available at home or that are inexpensive to buy. We're not as interested in providing directions for the "perfect" project as we are in encouraging children to become independent, creative thinkers.

Why are we so presumptuous as to think programs like ours can make a difference? Research tells us that children can reach out to the audience. Tests show that children, when invited to do so, will answer questions directly asked of them by a personality on a television program. When encouraged by a friendly well-trained host, they will even participate in the activities of that program. We can take advantage of that rapport to ask kids not just to jump up and down or clap their hands with children in the studio; we can also involve them in activities that teach cognitive skills, artistic skills, and language skills. Since most parents are not trained to be teachers, we like to think that children at home can learn something from our instruction—and have fun at the same time.

Romper Room has been on the air since 1953, but it's curious to note that the show fits in in its own way with the current television craze for "real people." The format of *Romper Room* depends on real live kids doing and saying what real live kids do and say, whether we want them to or not! We may plan before the show is taped for all five kids in the studio to do "X," but there is almost always one ornery someone who says, "That's dumb!" or "I don't want to!" There are no retakes. And that's the way the world is, if not the way we wish it to be.

Although participation is the cornerstone of our philosophy of producing "active television," we also recognize that TV is essentially an entertainment medium. We use puppets, film clips, props, whatever media we think we need to keep the children at home interested. We know we have to entertain in order to teach.

Just because we have been on the air for so long, we are constantly challenged to keep our thinking current, not to repeat, and to try to find new ways to reach preschoolers. That search is to me the creative part of my work: conceiving new things to do, developing innovative techniques to present material that is both informative and entertaining.

One of our most successful efforts has been our recent series of filmed segments focused on "economic education" for preschoolers. The term sounds lofty, but the concepts we present are rock-bottom fundamentals. To illustrate depletion of our natural resources, for example, I climbed aboard a two-person helicopter in Idaho and then landed in a clearing where many trees had been felled. Visuals like these narrated by a familiar face (in this case, mine!) are used to start a discussion on the *Romper Room* set (and, hopefully, to raise questions among viewers at home).

When we talked about trees, the kids came up with many examples of products made from wood—the paper and pencils they use at school, for example. While we talked, I asked them to watch a TV monitor showing a forest. Each time a child mentioned a wood product, some of the trees disappeared. By the time they had listed toys, houses, baseball bats, and so on, the trees were all gone. It was then only a tiny step for the kids to grasp the idea that to save trees, we had to use less wood. As the children volunteered suggestions ("use your pencil down to the eraser!"), the trees began to reappear on the screen.

Our tree series also includes segments on redwoods, prefab housing, logging, how plywood is made, and what goes on at a sawmill. Most of these films are about a minute long; some run as long as four minutes, some as short as twenty seconds. But all have the same intention: to take advantage of television's ability to bring the outside world into a child's home. Film makes it possible for us to involve our audience in experiences a parent couldn't duplicate at home.

In the search for dramatic or picturesque settings to clarify abstract concepts, I've been constantly on the road. Down the shaft of a silver mine in Utah (mineral resources). Into the control tower of Chicago's O'Hare airport (airplane transportation). On a banana boat in the Mississippi River (water transportation). In lettuce fields in California (farming). Our focus in these segments has been on the workers, on how their services and produced goods contribute to our economy. The pictures help kids to understand where things come from and how they are recycled into our daily lives.

We've discovered that talking to the workers inevitably exposes the kids who watch the segments to a kind of career education. In the farming series we meet a family of migrant lettuce pickers, visit a farmer who is the third generation in his family to raise wheat, watch a veterinarian treat baby animals. The films show something about how these people live as well as what they do. In the airplane series I take a spin in a flight simulator to give kids an insight into the rigors of pilot training. And a chat with an O'Hare air-traffic controller demonstrates that above all, a person in this occupation has to keep calm!

Now we are developing a new series about nutrition. Again we are emphasizing participation by presenting a number of no-bake recipes kids can prepare safely in their own kitchens. Since it's more fun to have a baker show you how to knead bread (and to eat it) than to be lectured by a teacher-type like me about food groups, we're finding food makers to appear on the program. We're also taking a tip from show business. We're utilizing a specially constructed robot named "Nutro" to maximize the impact of nutrition education messages. Because the robot is unusual and entertaining, kids who watch him are fascinated. When "Nutro" talks about shiny hair and bright eyes, kids are spellbound—remembering every word he says.

Romper Room has always had its share of media coverage. *Life* magazine helped us celebrate our tenth anniversary, *People* magazine our twenty-fifth. Newspaper and TV reporters visit our studios from time to time to find out what we're doing (and usually to ponder why we have stayed on the air so long). But we have all been surprised by the spurt of articles spawned by our series on economic education. After *The Wall Street Journal* described our series in a feature story (March 7, 1980), a dubious New York *Times* reporter (March 20, 1980) followed up with phone calls to some of the five-year-olds who had been on the show. His story reported that not only did kids understand such concepts as goods and services, but that they remembered what they had learned as well. *Canadian Business* (October 1980) then incorporated our experiment into a longer piece about educating kids to handle money in a capitalist economy—especially in times of inflation.

That kind of enthusiastic response, especially from skeptics, is what has kept us going for twenty-nine years, making *Romper Room* the longest-running children's program on television. Early on we chose not to be a network show and risk sudden cancellation; instead we have survived by going the syndication route, an option that has enabled us to adapt our format to the particular cities in which the show appears. That ability to customize is why *Romper Room* is sometimes hosted by different teachers in certain areas.

We know from statistics and from letters from our viewers that something about what we do works. More than 1.4 million children watch *Romper Room* five times a week in forty-five U.S. cities, Canada, New Zealand, Australia,

Thailand, Borneo, and Japan. Many of our letters are charming notes from children ("I loved it when you kissed the porpoise!"). Some are requests from kindergarten teachers ("Could you please repeat the directions for making a home balance beam?"). Surprisingly, some are from prisoners ("I like to watch the show because the kids remind me of my own kids."), or from older retired people ("I just enjoy seeing the children do things.").

But most of our letters are from supportive parents. The mother of one little girl who lives in a rural area without nearby playmates wrote us to say how important the show was to her child to watch other children doing things. Another mother of a little boy living in a city wrote us to say her child had skipped first grade. Of course, there is always the outrageous complaint ("Your program teaches violence! Punch and Judy are violent!") or ("I've been trying to get my child on *Romper Room* for two years with no success!").

That kids at home do respond to the kids in the studio is indicated by the many, many requests we receive to appear on the show. In the cities where *Romper Room* is aired, we generally have a waiting list of over a year for children who want to be on the program. A good number of these are second-generation "legacies," kids whose parents were on the show twenty years ago

and whose mother or daddy wants them to enjoy a similar experience. Then there are always the parents who just want to be able to say that their child was on TV. But most of the parents tell us they simply want their child to be able to participate.

No matter how successful we think *Romper Room* is now, no matter how we break our necks to make it a better show in the future, we in the television industry must always face the reality that we are in a competitive business. A children's program like ours will always be up against stiff rivalry from cartoons, particularly in those early-morning hours. There's no denying cartoons are fun for kids to watch. And market research tells us that given the option, children will choose cartoons over any other program.

But sometimes parents can't permit that option. As Dorothy Singer at Yale has pointed out, literary criticism begins with preschoolers; even the youngest child can practice "thinking about what you are seeing"—if he is urged to do so.

Fads in television come and go, but with *Romper Room* we try to provide an option for action. In these "back-to-basics" times, our format seems to have endured. In the ups and downs of our business, something persists. Perhaps it's the mutual need of parents and kids for ideas of things to do together at home that never goes out of style.

INDEX